World Trends in Life Insurance

World Trends in Life Insurance

STEPHEN WYNN

A HALSTED PRESS BOOK

JOHN WILEY & SONS
New York – Toronto

English language edition, except USA, published by
Associated Business Programmes Ltd
17 Buckingham Gate, London SW1

Published in the USA and Canada by
Halsted Press, a Division
of John Wiley & Sons, Inc
New York

First published 1975

Library of Congress Cataloging in Publication Data

Wynn, Stephen.
World trends in life insurance.

"A Halsted Press book."
Bibliography: p.
Includes index.
1. Insurance, Life. I. Title.
HG8771.W93 1975 368.3′2 75-16231
ISBN 0–470–96903–2

This book has been printed in Great Britain
by The Anchor Press Ltd, and bound by
Wm Brendon & Son Ltd, both of Tiptree, Essex

Contents

LIST OF DIAGRAMS

LIST OF TABLES

Acknowledgements

This study was financed by a grant from the Social Science Research Council, and was written during nineteen months at the Department of Economics of the University of Essex, under the supervision of Professor C. J. Bliss. During this time I had the good fortune to meet Professor R. E. Beard who generously provided extensive help and guidance by means of weekly discussions and criticisms of my manuscripts. He introduced me to his colleagues in the insurance industry and, in particular, to experts from many different countries at an annual meeting of ASTIN at the University of Essex at which he was host. I am indebted to Mr Sidney Benjamin for his comments on an early draft and also to Mr Michael Gordon who came to see me on several occasions and supplied me with useful material. The Association Internationale pour l'Etude de l'Economie de l'Assurance paid for the publication by the award of the Ernst Meyer Prize. The Association also provided help by asking three of its advisers to read two drafts of the text; and I am grateful to Professor R. L. Carter, Professor H. A. L. Cockerell and Mr P. R. T. Jones for their comments. Mr Jones also went through the final text with me in detail. To all the people who have helped me I would like to express my gratitude and especially to Professor Bliss and Professor Beard.

Preface

We live in an era of social change. Our views on 'fairness' and 'equality' are changing rapidly, probably more rapidly than at any other time in our history. There is a continuous re-appraisal of the relationships between one sector of society and another, particularly the relationships between companies and other sectors of society. The concept of 'social accountability' has become an accepted part of our industrial and commercial life.

The life assurance industry is not immune from these pressures. Indeed, it is healthy that its role in society should be continuously re-assessed for it is only in this way that it can fully meet the demands of the Society it seeks to serve. However, the highly complex nature of the industry and the equally complex nature of the legislation surrounding the industry serve to deter the majority from attempting to analyse the industry's role.

Most research in the past has been undertaken by people employed within the industry. People whose close involvement with life assurance makes it difficult for them to see the industry through the eyes of other sectors of society. It is against this background that the Association Internationale pour l'Etude de l'Economie de l'Assurance seeks to encourage original research, and against which it is particularly pleased to have been able to contribute to this particular work by awarding the author the Ernst Meyer Prize.

The book discusses the major relationships between life assurance and several other sectors of society including competing financial institutions, the consumer and the government. By comparing the experience of several countries the author has been able to propose a number of changes which he feels would be desirable. The background of rapid change mentioned above means that there will inevitably be some who disagree with the author's conclusions. It is to be hoped that those who do disagree will be prompted to publish their own views since the life assurance industry can only benefit from informed discussion of its function in the modern world. In the meantime this book presents the views of someone not employed within the life assurance industry which will provide refreshing, stimulating reading for those who are interested in the future of life assurance.

Association Internationale pour l'Etude de l'Economie de l'Assurance: 18, chemin Rieu, 1208 Geneva.

24·3·75

Introduction

The development of the business of life insurance companies generally represents progress for policyholders resulting, for example, from a greater efficiency in the operation of business, an improved visibility of the rates of return provided and an improved visibility of the charges made by companies for their services. However, such progress may be unintentionally held up by government regulations. The development of new kinds of business such as linked life assurance often requires new regulations, and these may bring into question the existing regulations for traditional business.

Life assurance policies can contain a small or large saving component relative to the amount of insurance protection provided, according to the design of the policy. There is no natural division between life assurance policies and saving schemes since, as the amount of insurance component in a life assurance policy reduces to zero, it becomes in effect a saving scheme. Divisions are created by regulations which necessarily tend to be rather complex and arbitrary. However, such divisions are needed when life assurance policies are provided with special regulations compared with saving schemes concerning for example taxation and commission payments to brokers.

The growth of business for group life insurance and linked life assurance are aspects of a trend towards the separation of personal saving and life insurance. On the one hand, the growth of group life insurance may be seen as a pooling of insurance risks and, on the other hand, linked life assurance is based on the division of the risks resulting from the fluctuating value of investments. Both these trends relate to an improved visibility of expense charges. The pooling of risks is intrinsic to the nature of insurance whereas the same concept applied to investment risks produces the problems of equity between savers which are described in chapter 5. The trend towards group life insurance may be unintentionally inhibited by providing larger tax concessions for individual policies than for group life schemes.

CHAPTER 1

The Erosion of the Traditional Differences between Life Insurance Companies and other Financial Institutions

A variety of developments such as increased mechanisation and an increased use of bank accounts, have tended to widen the activities of different kinds of financial institutions including commercial banks, savings banks, building societies, credit cooperatives and life insurance companies, and thereby have reduced the differences between them as they encroach on each other's territory.[1]

The remarkable growth of share prices during the 1950s as shown on diagram 1 greatly increased the popularity of investment in shares and promoted the rapid growth of open-ended funds such as unit trusts in the United Kingdom and mutual funds in the United States. Various 'equity products' were developed by life insurance companies to take advantage of this enthusiasm, and insured pension schemes tended to adopt the form of a managed portfolio of investments. In general, therefore, there has been an

[1]The activities of financial institutions in EEC countries were studied in *The Development of a European Capital Market*, by the EEC Commission (1966). It states (para 8, p. 271): 'In each of the EEC countries there is a growing tendency for each type of financial intermediary to enlarge its range of activity, both in the collection and in the employment of funds. This trend seems to be a fundamental one and is accepted by the national authorities.'

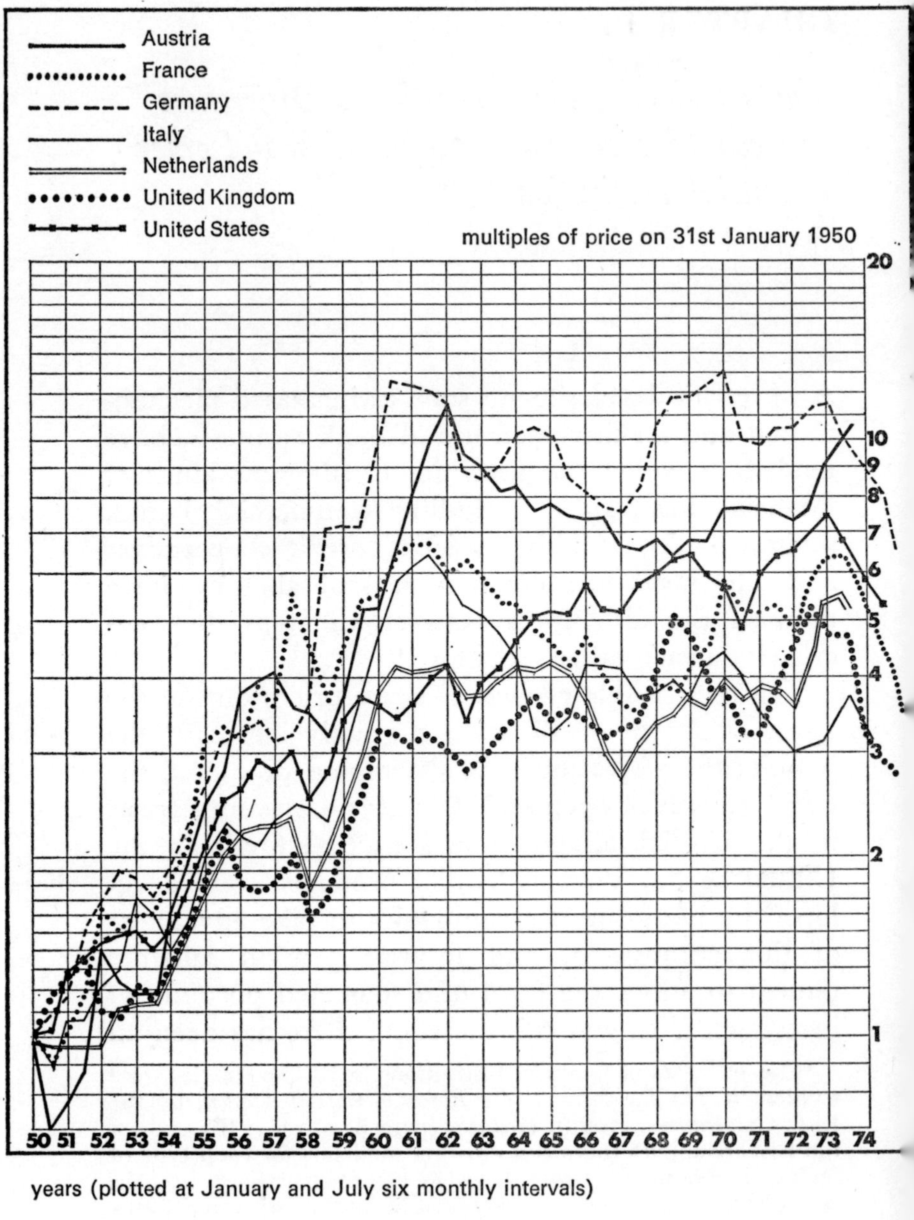

DIAGRAM I

SHARE PRICES IN SEVEN COUNTRIES 1950–73

increase in the business of portfolio management whether of unit trust funds, pension funds or funds supporting some kind of equity product, and there has been a corresponding increase in the competition between financial institutions for the management of portfolios of different kinds. Since the Second World War the proportion of the assets of financial institutions held in shares has also greatly increased. These trends are discussed in the classic study on the investment policies of financial institutions in the United States, the *Institutional Investor Study Report*:[1]

> Different classes of institutional investors formerly competed with one another for the saver's dollar only weakly. Bank trust departments, insurance companies and investment companies each offered relatively distinct types of financial services aimed at largely non-overlapping classes of customers and markets. Shifts toward increased equity investment by most types of institutions, however, have tended to erode traditional differences between respective markets and heighten the degree of competition not only within but also across institutional categories for the management of various types of portfolios.

The rapid post-Second World War growth of unit trusts in the United Kingdom and mutual funds in the United States and of open-ended funds in West Germany is shown in diagrams 2, 3 and 4. These diagrams show the total assets of different financial institutions (on a logarithmic scale) and thus illustrate their relative success in attracting investment. Particularly impressive has been the growth of open-ended

[1]Securities and Exchange Commission (1971), Vol. 1, p. xii.

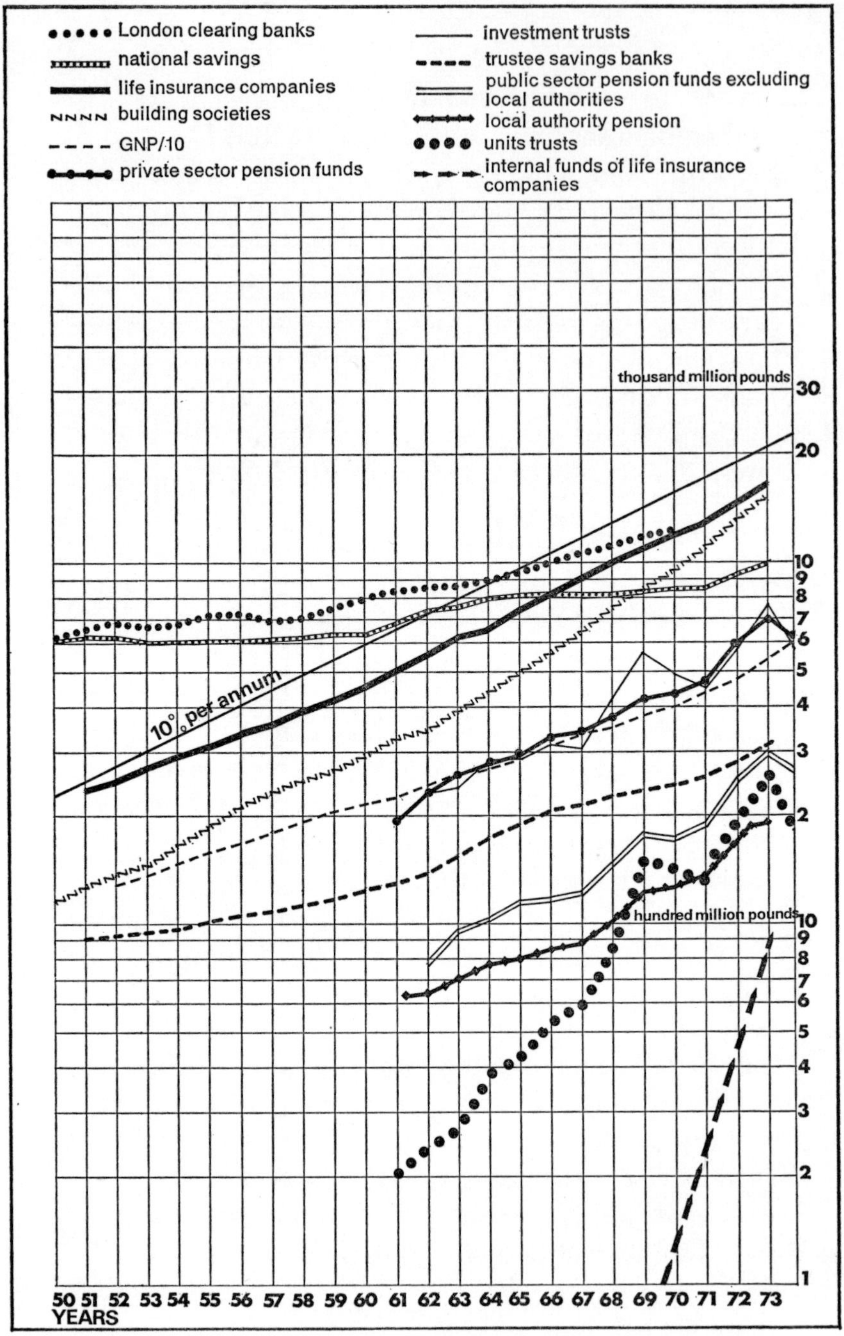

DIAGRAM 2

THE TOTAL ASSETS OF FINANCIAL INSTITUTIONS IN THE UNITED KINGDOM: 1950–73

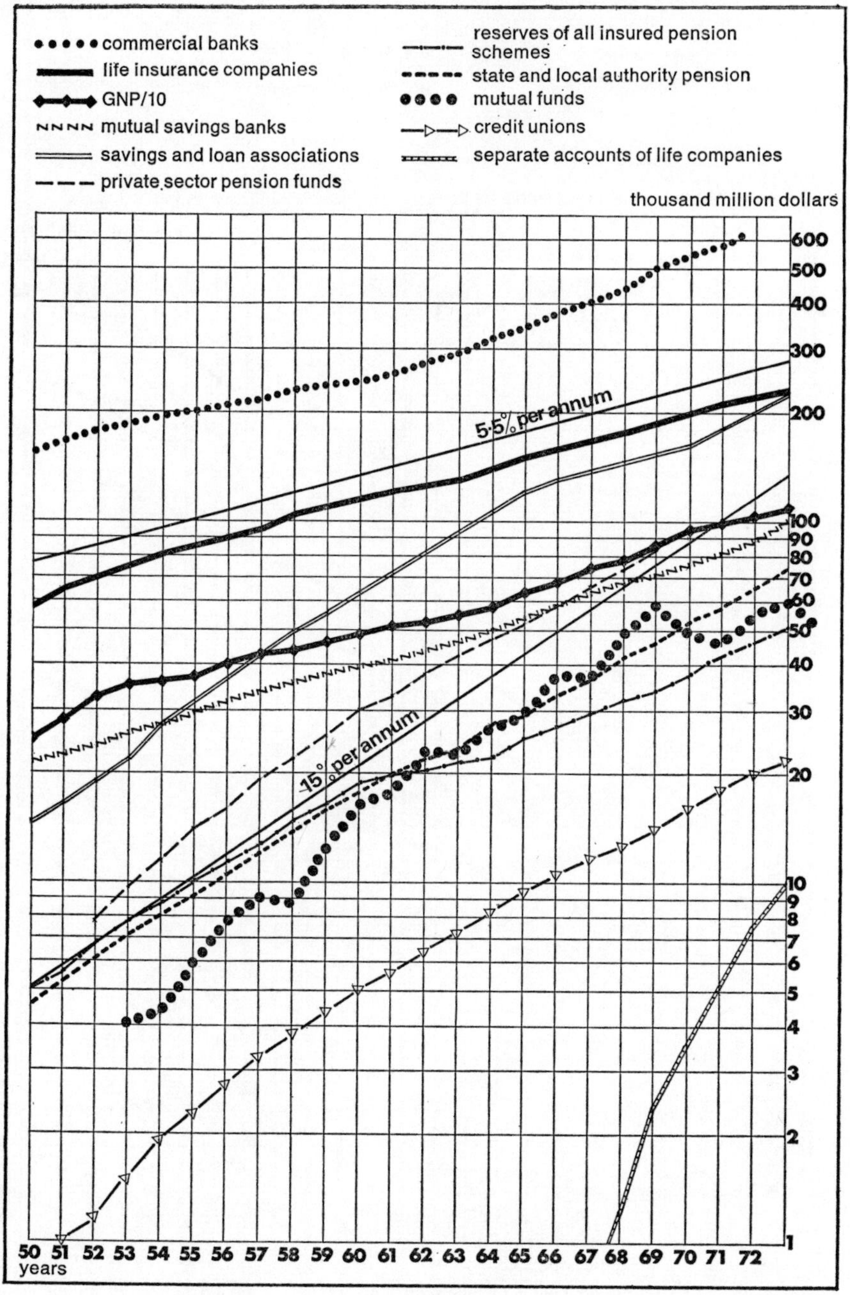

DIAGRAM 3

THE TOTAL ASSETS OF FINANCIAL INSTITUTIONS IN THE UNITED STATES 1950–73

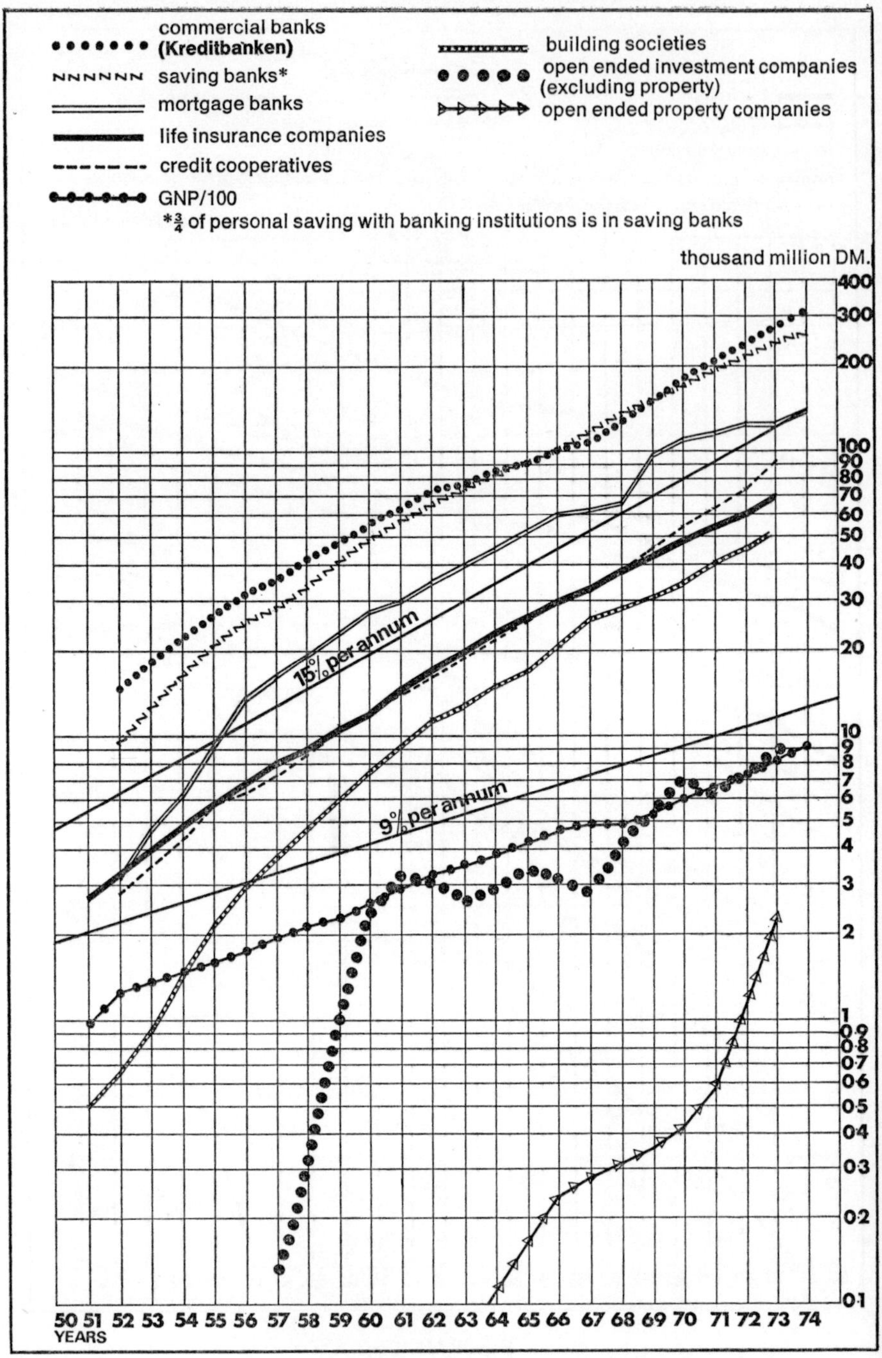

DIAGRAM 4

THE TOTAL ASSETS OF FINANCIAL INSTITUTIONS IN WEST GERMANY: 1950–73

funds in France known as SICAV.[1] The first of these funds was launched in 1964 after the necessary legislation had been passed. By the end of 1969 their assets were nearly F10 billion, and by 1973 exceeded F20 billion.

Diagram 3 shows that the assets of life insurance companies in the United States have been growing at about 5·5 per cent per annum since 1950, whereas those of savings and loan associations, private pension funds, mutual funds and credit unions have been growing at about 15 per cent for most of the same period. In Canada life insurance companies have also encountered fierce competition from mutual funds.[2]

The proportion of the assets of life insurance companies held in shares and in commercial property in the years 1950, 1960 and 1972 is shown in table I, which indicates remarkably uniform increases in these proportions in different countries. Diagrams 5 and 6 show the proportions of the assets of various financial institutions in the United Kingdom and the United States held in shares in the years from 1950 for which data are available. These diagrams also demonstrate a steady increase in share investments. One reason for the varying proportions of assets invested in shares between different countries is the existence of government regulations restricting investment activity. Such restrictions always fall heaviest on share and

[1]Société d'investissement à capital variable.

[2]A paper at the 19th International Congress of Actuaries (1972) (Vol., 1 p. 577), reported: 'Canadian life assurance companies grew from $4 billion a year end 1950 to $6·5 billion at year end 1961: the assets of mutual funds grew from about $46 million in 1950 to $795 million in 1961. From 1961 to 1967, the assets of life insurance companies almost doubled while those of mutual funds more than tripled.'

TABLE I

THE PERCENTAGE OF THE INVESTMENTS OF LIFE INSURANCE COMPANIES HELD IN SHARES AND PROPERTY, IN THIRTEEN COUNTRIES: 1950, 1960 AND 1972

	Shares[1]			*Property*[1]		
Country	*1950*	*1960*	*1972*	*1950*	*1960*	*1972*
Australia	7·7[2]	14·3[2]	16·2	—	—	16·3
Belgium	5·6	5·8	5·6	3·7	6·3	12·8
Canada	3·1	4·0	11·1	1·6	3·2	5·5
Denmark	0·6	2·7	9·7	2·5	3·1	5·3
France	n.a.	n.a.	23·4	4·9	7·1	11·3
Germany	n.a.	n.a.	5·4	2·4	10·2	13·5
Italy	n.a.	4·6	6·3	n.a.	43·5	44·4
Netherlands	3·8	3·2	5·6	6·4	7·4	7·6
Norway	0·4	0·5	1·2	0·8	1·7	2·9
Sweden	1·1	3·7	3·6	2·5	4·3	5·5
Switzerland	n.a.	n.a.	1·1	8·3	14.2	21·7
United Kingdom	11·1	21·9	28·6	5·7	10·1	13·9
United States	3·3	4·2	11·2	2·2	3·1	3·0

[1]Balance sheet (book) values.
[2]Including property.

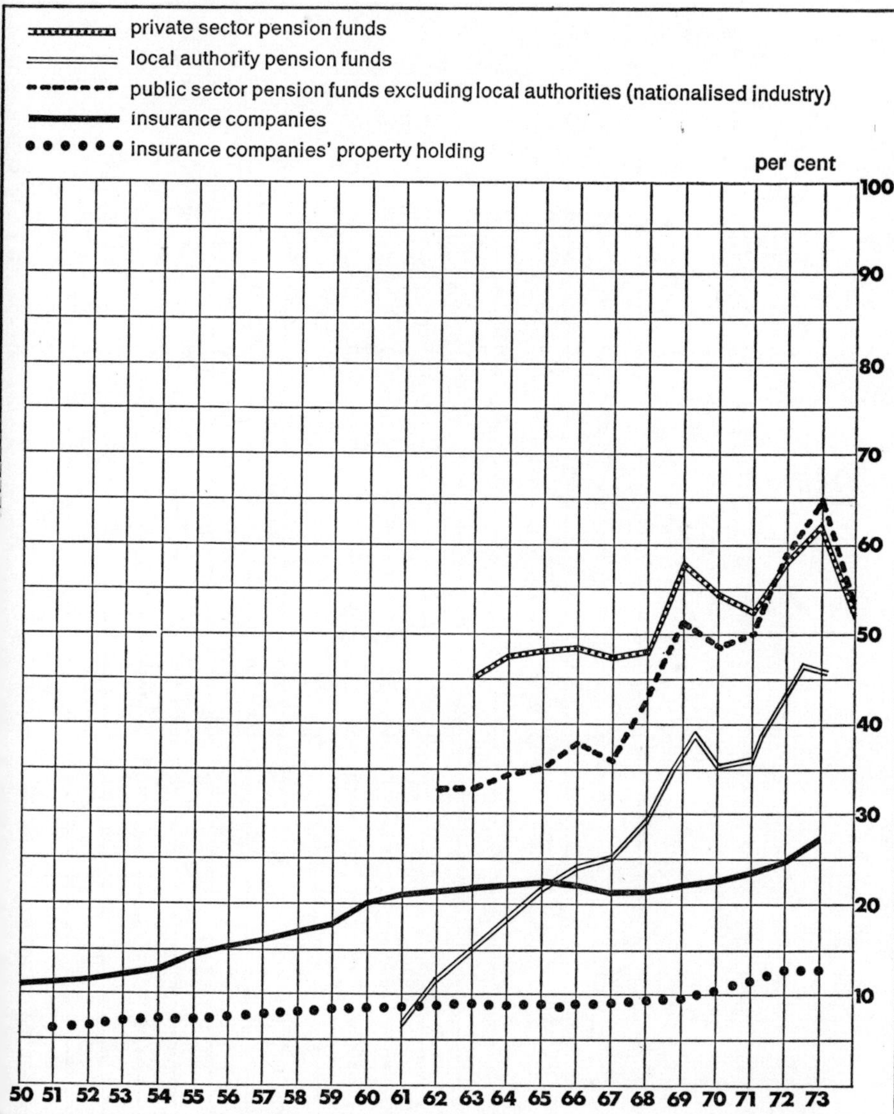

DIAGRAM 5

THE PERCENTAGE OF THE ASSETS OF FINANCIAL INSTITUTIONS IN THE UNITED KINGDOM WHICH ARE INVESTED IN SHARES: 1950–73

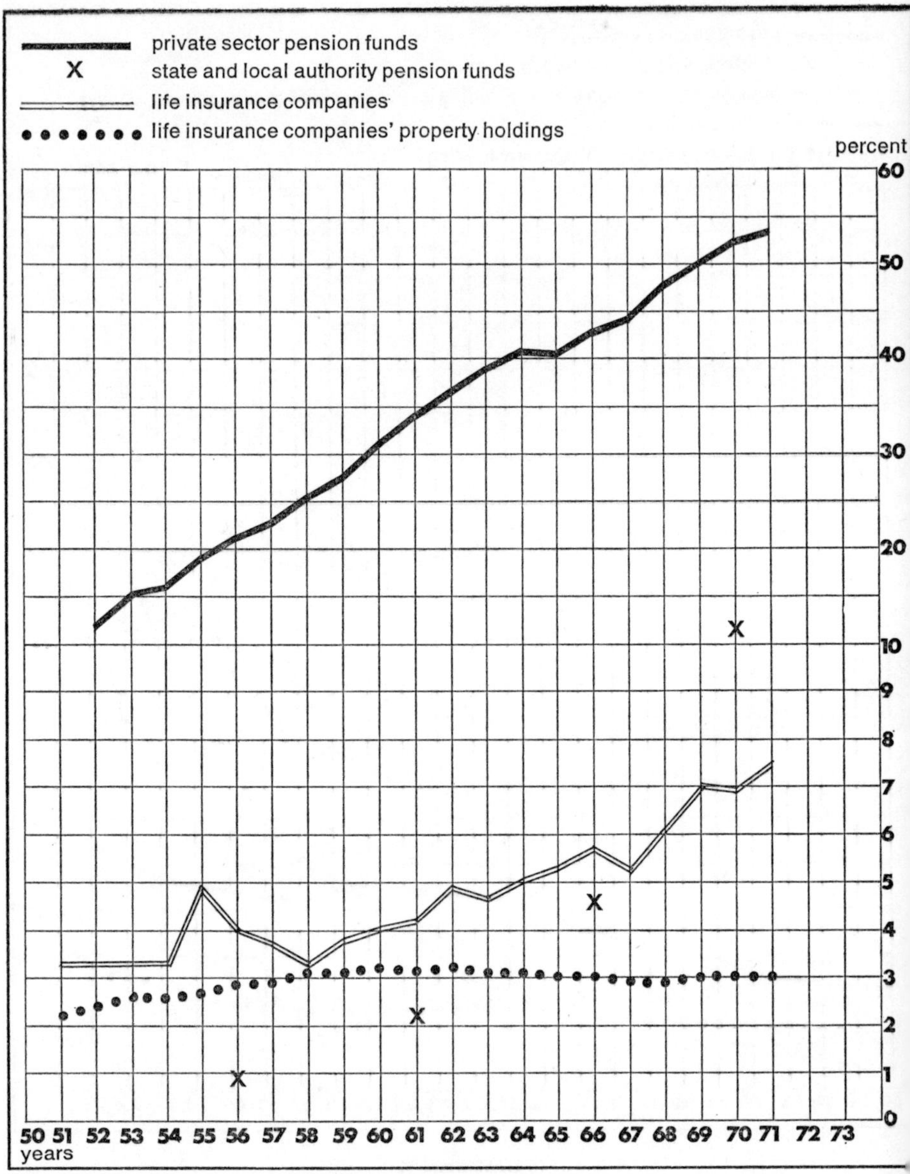

DIAGRAM 6

THE PERCENTAGE OF THE ASSETS OF FINANCIAL INSTITUTIONS IN THE UNITED STATES WHICH ARE INVESTED IN SHARES: 1950–71

property investments whereas financial institutions are always free to invest in government bonds, and indeed may be obliged to do so. The closer a financial institution or organisation is to government, the more it tends to be restricted in its investment activity. For example, prior to the 1961 Trustee Investments Act, in the United Kingdom local authorities could not invest their pension fund money in shares. In the United States, state and local authority pension funds have been subjected to severe investment restrictions, although these are now gradually being removed. The civil service retirement system in the United States has a pension fund of $25 thousand million (at June 1971) entirely invested in government bonds (with an actuarial deficit of $58 thousand million).

Life insurance companies in the United Kingdom have a higher proportion of their assets invested in shares compared with those of other countries. The proportion shown in table I for 1972 is 28·6 per cent. This represents book values; including market values this figure would have increased to possibly as much as 40 per cent. There are no restrictions on the investment activity of life insurance companies in the United Kingdom such as exist in most other countries. These limitations are sometimes quite complex but some information about them is given in table II. However, since the Second World War they have been gradually reduced. For example, a rule requiring life insurance companies in France to invest 50 per cent of statutory reserves in 'first category' investments was replaced in 1972 by a ruling that only 33 per cent of the reserves had to be in bonds. The 'first category' investments were originally entirely government and local authority bonds but over the years the bonds of various deserving organisations were included. This rule dates from 1938—just before the war and the resulting severe inflation.

The increase in share and property investments

TABLE II

THE PERCENTAGE OF THE ASSETS OF LIFE INSURANCE COMPANIES WHICH MAY BE HELD IN SHARES AND PROPERTY, IN ELEVEN COUNTRIES[1]

Country	*Shares*	*Property*
Australia[2]	70 together	
Belgium[3]	25	65
Canada[4]	25	10
Denmark	16 together	
France[5]	50 together	
Germany[6]	15	25
Netherlands	no restrictions	
Norway	15 together	
Sweden	none	none
United Kingdom	no restrictions	
United States[7]	varies between states	

[1]Summary of the regulations described at the 19th International Congress of Actuaries in 1972. The figures are generally percentages of the *statutory reserves*, that is the assets legally required to cover the liabilities resulting from life and pension business. This may not be the same as the total assets.

[2]30 per cent must be in public sector securities to qualify for certain tax concessions.

[3]15 per cent must be in public sector securities.

[4]The 10 per cent for property may be increased in certain special circumstances.

[5]Changed from 50 per cent to 67 per cent in December 1972.

[6]The 25 per cent for property may be increased if special permission is obtained.

[7]Legislation in most states following the 1906 Armstrong Committee Report prohibited share and property investments, but since the Second World War there has been a gradual easing of this restriction and in most states up to 10 or 15 per cent of reserves may be held in shares and another 10 or 15 per cent in property.

reflects a generally more dynamic investment philosophy. This was expressed by the vice-president of the New York Stock Exchange in a 1971 paper.[1]

> Decades ago it was an accepted principle of sound institutional investment management to pick high-grade, blue-chip type securities, stash them away in a safe deposit box, and review the portfolio every few years. All this has changed drastically.

It is convenient to distinguish between three different kinds of portfolios of investments managed by life insurance companies. First there are the open-ended funds such as unit trusts in the United Kingdom and mutual funds in the United States. Life insurance companies have moved strongly into this business in recent years,[2] generally by means of the establishment of subsidiary management companies.

Second, there are portfolios of investments which come under insurance company regulations and which are divided into units on the same principle as unit trusts. These portfolios are known in the United Kingdom as 'internal funds'. They support either variable annuity or linked life assurance business. Under variable annuity policies, the units, generally called 'accumulation units', accumulated before retirement. The units of the internal funds for linked life

[1]Paper given at the Wharton School of Finance and Commerce (1971), p. 110.

[2]For example, the Prudential Unit Trust was launched in 1968, and the Pearl-Montague Unit Trust in 1969. Nearly all life insurance companies in the United Kingdom now have some kind of affiliation with unit trusts. For the United States see Kannel, C., 'Rush to Mutual Funds by Insurance Companies Approaches Stampede,' *Wall Street Journal*, 25 February 1970.

assurance business are known as 'property bonds', 'managed bonds' or 'equity bonds', according to how the funds are invested, managed bond funds being a combination of shares, property and fixed interest investments. Property bonds were introduced in 1965. They provide a means of applying the open-ended or unit-trust principle to property investment. Unit trusts in the United Kingdom are not allowed to purchase property. Property bonds enable small savers to participate directly in the ownership of commercial property without having to buy the shares of property companies on the stock market, and property bond funds amounted to £572 million in April 1974. Managed bonds were introduced in 1971, and are a natural extension of the property bond idea io include share investments. Managed bond funds amounted to £359 million in April 1974.[1]

The growth of the number of level premium linked life assurance policies in the United Kingdom is shown in diagram 7. About half of these policies are linked to unit trusts, with the rest linked to internal funds, except for a comparatively small number linked to building society accounts. The total premium income from these policies in 1973 was £121 million compared with £739 million and £377 million of premium income from traditional level premium policies of the ordinary and industrial branches respectively. The total income from the premiums of single premium policies, practically all of which is linked life assurance, has grown from £27 million in

[1]Estimates of *Money Management*, May 1974. The £572 million includes £116 million of managed bond money invested in property.

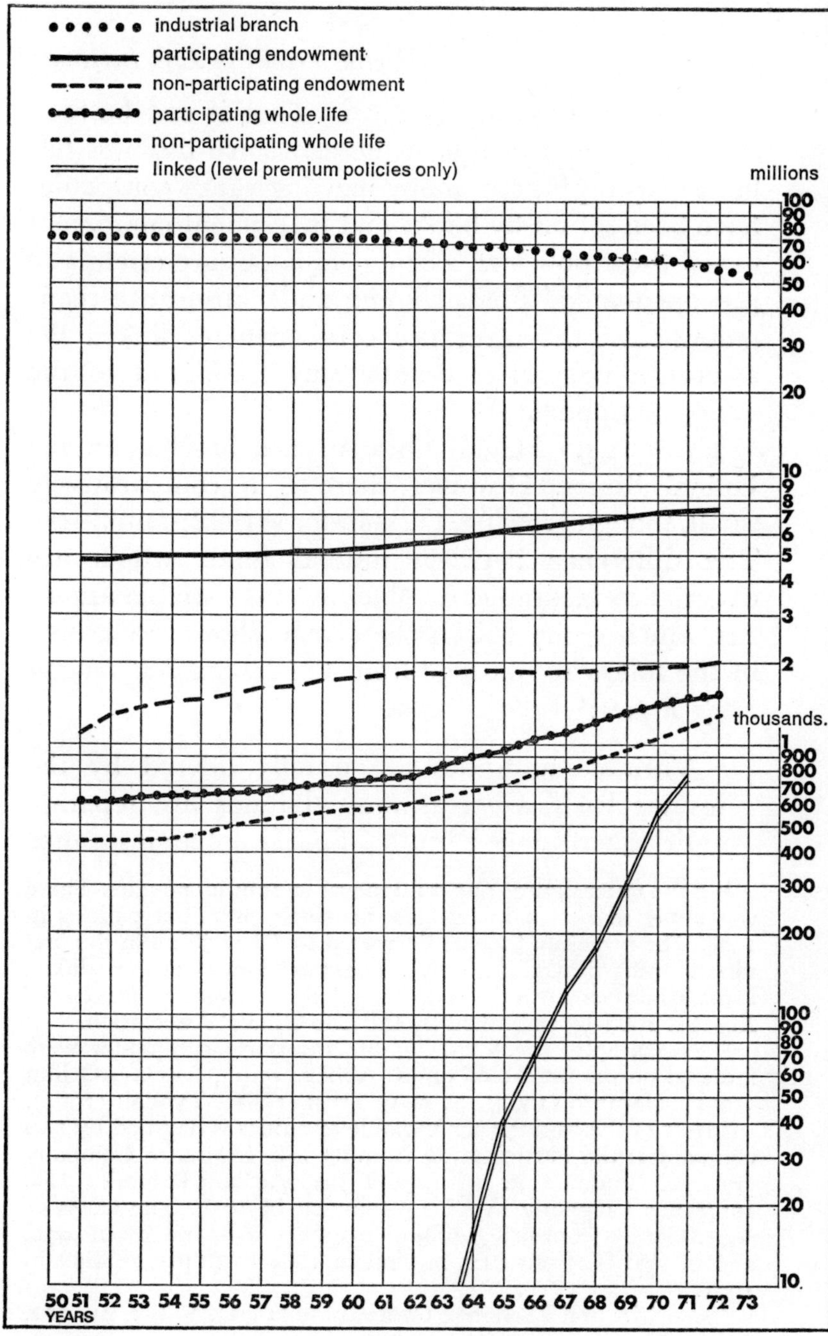

DIAGRAM 7

THE NUMBER OF LIFE ASSURANCE POLICIES OF DIFFERENT KINDS IN THE UNITED KINGDOM: 1950–72.

1969 to £346 million in 1973.[1] Thus it can be seen that the growth of linked life assurance business has been very rapid, and many new insurance companies have been set up by banks and investment companies to sell these policies.[2] These companies are essentially just open-ended funds coming under insurance regulations since the insurance component of linked life assurance policies is usually tiny compared to the saving component.

There is no linked life assurance business in the United States. However there is a comparatively small, though growing, business for variable annuities.[3] The difference between mutual funds which are external to insurance regulations and variable annuities which come within these regulations is clarified in the following passage from the *Institutional Investor Study Report*:[4]

> Variable annuities are usually offered by the insurer itself, whereas mutual funds are separate entities, and since a mutual fund is not an insurance

[1]Of the latter figure, £25 million was in annuity policies. There was a big reduction in business for single premium policies in 1974. The premium income decreased to £85 million in the first nine months (linked life only). These are figures of the Linked Life Assurance Group, and from *Life Assurance in the United Kingdom* 1969–73 published by the Life Offices' Association.

[2]For example, the following life insurance companies were founded on the bracketed dates: Abbey (1961), Barclays Griffin (1971), Hambro (1965), M & G Trust (1961), Tyndall (1964).

[3]Most of the business for variable annuities is handled by two companies; the Participating Annuity Life Insurance Company (PALIC) founded in 1954, and the Variable Annuity Life Insurance Company (VALIC) founded in 1953. The assets of VALIC grew from $18·3 million in 1965 to $187 million in 1972, and of PALIC from $1·5 million in 1964 to $146·3 million in 1971.

[4]Securities and Exchange Commission (1971), Vol. 2, pp. 522, 534.

product, the only state regulatory problem is usually that of obtaining statutory authorisation to establish the necessary subsidiaries. The authorisation was provided to New York companies only in late 1969. Variable annuities, on the other hand, may create more federal-state regulatory conflicts since they are securities for purposes of application of federal securities laws and are regulated as insurance products by the state insurance departments.

Because of the heated disagreement in the insurance industry over the appropriateness of the variable annuity as an insurance product and, perhaps, because of the long litigation over the applicability of the federal securities laws, many states enacted the necessary authorising legislation only late in the 1960s.

The third kind of portfolio administered by life insurance companies is the pension scheme known in the United Kingdom as the 'managed fund', and in the United States as the 'separate account'. The total assets in the separate accounts in the United States are shown in diagram 3 and in diagram 9. It can be seen that the separate accounts have been growing rapidly. Similarly, in the United Kingdom there has been a rapid growth of business for the managed fund. The development of this business was discussed at a 1972 meeting of the Institute of Actuaries on insured pension schemes. The President, Mr G. Heywood, said:[1]

> I find it difficult to believe that as recently as 1951 group deferred annuity policies in the UK were

[1] Fellows (1972), p. 66.

written entirely in non-profit form. The commencement of with profits contracts shortly afterwards was indeed a mile-stone and had led to the development of sophisticated techniques such as controlled funding and deposit administration. When looking back in 1991 I believe that the introduction of the managed fund, which has taken place some three or four years ago, will be an even greater milestone than that of the introduction of with profits policies because with this latest development the last difference between the old insured scheme and the privately invested fund has finally disappeared, and both have become almost identical except for the medium of investment. I believe that the next ten years, if not perhaps the next five years, will see the managed fund virtually replace insured schemes as we know them, with the result that the whole emphasis will be more and more on investment and less and less on insurance.

The management of portfolios is, of course, a different business from the provision of life insurance. The extent to which the life insurance companies of different countries provide insurance coverage rather than a vehicle for saving can be seen by the statistics derived from the ratio: total life insurance in force[1]/

[1]'Total life insurance in force' is the total sum insured under ordinary, industrial and group business. It may or may not also include pension business and annuities, but this imperfection in the definition, due to different accounting conventions in different countries, makes little difference to the ratios. The US *Life Insurance Fact Book* gives the total life insurance in force as a percentage of national income in 1971 as follows: Canada 184, USA 176, Sweden 156, New Zealand 149, Japan 149, Australia 131, Netherlands 127, UK 113, Switzerland 75, France 55, Denmark 54, Belgium 52, Germany 48, Norway 43, Finland 34, Brazil 23, Italy 16.

total assets of life companies, or total life insurance in force/total annual premium payments. The former ratio for the United States in 1972 was 7·3 whereas for the United Kingdom it was 3·1. The larger figure for the United States was due to the large proportion of group life business and the large proportion of whole life policies compared to endowment policies. In the United States life assurance policies are chiefly bought to provide life insurance cover whereas in the United Kingdom they are chiefly used for saving.

The business of life insurance companies can be roughly classified according to the extent of the insurance component in different policies compared to the saving component. Portfolio management as discussed above does not directly involve life insurance at all. Endowment policies contain a substantially larger saving component than whole life policies. Individual term insurance policies contain a very small saving component and group life insurance policies of the yearly renewable kind discussed in the next chapter contain essentially no saving component at all. In this chapter the trend towards portfolio management in the United Kingdom and United States has been discussed. On the other hand, the growth of group life insurance business discussed in the next chapter represents a trend in the opposite direction in the sense that it is a trend towards a type of policy with little or no savings component. The growth of linked life assurance, the designs of which are discussed in chapter 3, also reflects these two trends, since the savings component of these policies is usually a share of a managed portfolio of investments and the insurance component may be paid for by a group life insurance scheme.

CHAPTER 2

The Group Life Insurance Scheme versus the Individually Purchased Policy

The probability of someone dying in a particular year is influenced by many factors including age, health and occupation, and these factors influence the premium charges of individual life insurance policies. However, if a group of people are provided with life insurance cover of similar amounts in return for a lump sum premium payment, then the characteristics of individual members become merged into the characteristics of the group, so that the larger the group the less relevant is information about any particular member for the calculation of the premium charge. If a particular member of a large group falls ill, this will not significantly affect the insurance risks since some members of the group can be expected to be ill at any one time. This has the important consequence that the premium charge can be calculated at yearly intervals for each year's cover. Group life insurance is generally provided on such a yearly basis and is known as 'yearly renewable group term insurance', although 'group life insurance' is generally used in this sense. It is not practicable to have yearly premium assessment for individual policies because, apart from the administrative difficulties, there is the fundamental objection that should the policy-holder become ill the insurance company might increase his premium charge or be unwilling to renew his cover at a time when he needs it most.

Most group life business is for coverage of groups of employees and the death benefits are usually related to earnings. Important, also, are schemes for groups of creditors or mortgage holders. Group life insurance is particularly highly developed in the United States where there has been a general proliferation of the number of different kinds of groups covered since the Second World War. Various kinds of groups are listed by Gregg (1962) in his book on group life insurance, in which he mentions such curious groups as college alumni and purchasers of groceries.[1]

The essence of the group insurance concept is that all members pay equal contributions or contributions which are determined by criteria such as salary levels, and not to differences in health or risk hazards between members of the group. This means that the healthy are in effect helping the sick, and the young are helping the old. If the scheme is to continue in existence there has, therefore, to be an element of compulsory membership otherwise the healthier or younger members would leave the scheme as they could probably get cheaper cover elsewhere. There must be a sufficient element of solidarity between the members of the group to prevent membership being affected by the existence of the scheme. Thus there are

[1]'Among the special types of groups sometimes written by companies are correspondent bank employees, correspondent bank borrowers, savings and loan leagues, organisations of farmers, national organisation of investment bankers, members of a livestock exchange, reserve officer associations, alien contract labour groups, savings account plan depositors, and many others.' Gregg (1962), p. 66.

various criteria to which group life insurance schemes have to conform. Any considerable deviation from these criteria is likely to result in a special loading of the premium, thereby increasing the cost of the insurance cover. The various criteria are summarised in the following list (which is not definitive):

1. There is a particular group of people, defined by criteria unrelated to the existence of the scheme.
2. Membership of the scheme is compulsory for all members of the group (or at least membership covers a very high proportion of the group).
3. The death benefit for each member of the scheme is determined by criteria unrelated to his individual health or risk hazards.
4. The scheme is non-contributory, or at least contributions to the scheme by each member is determined by criteria unrelated to his individual health or risk hazards.
5. There is a reasonable age limit, such as sixty-five, for membership of the group.
6. The death benefit for a particular member of the scheme should not be very much larger than those of other members. The death benefits are for this reason usually subject to a maximum amount.
7. The group must be reasonably large (a common minimum size is twenty-five).

The total amounts of life insurance provided by different kinds of policy in the United States since 1940 are shown in diagram 8. It can be seen that the cover provided by group policies has been growing more rapidly than the cover provided by ordinary or industrial policies. The first group life insurance scheme

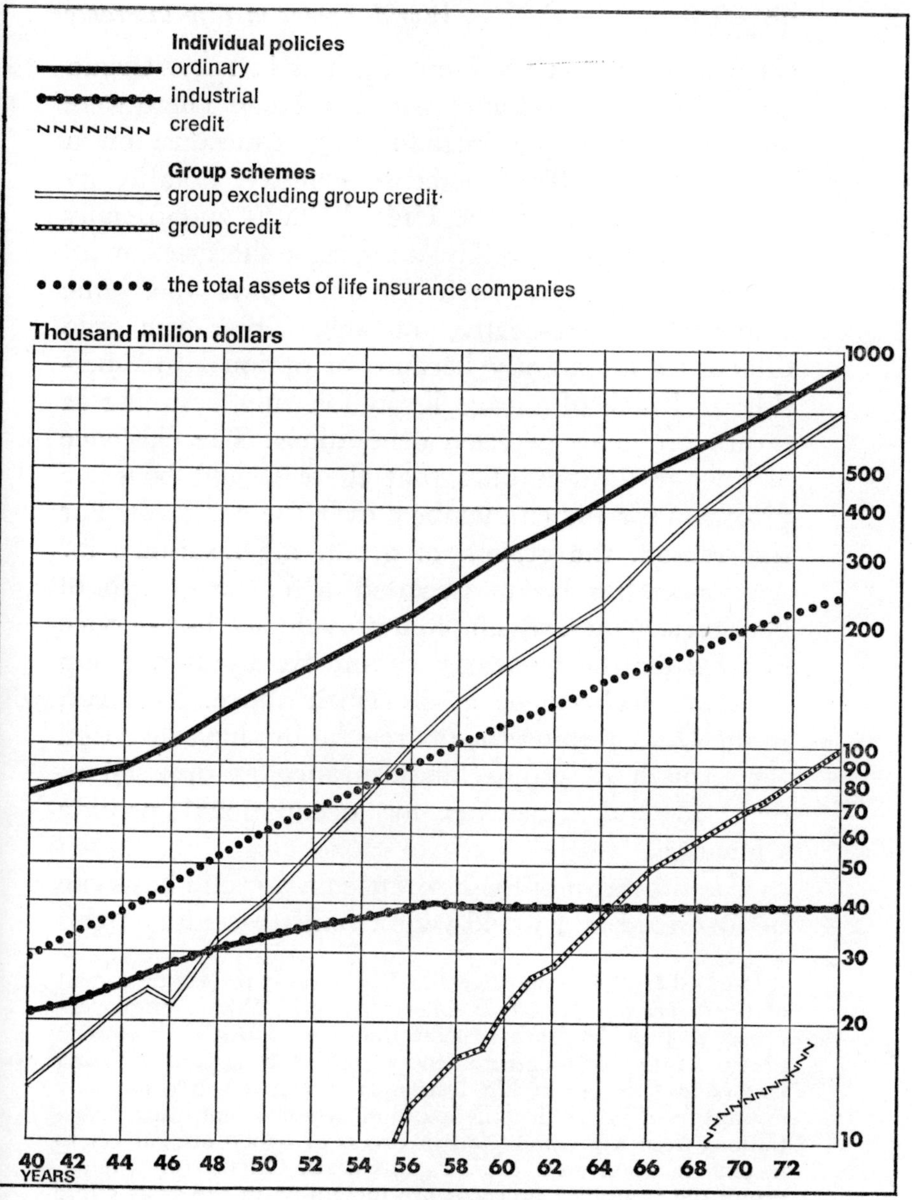

DIAGRAM 8

THE AMOUNT OF LIFE INSURANCE IN FORCE IN THE UNITED STATES UNDER INDIVIDUAL POLICIES AND GROUP LIFE INSURANCE SCHEMES: 1940–72.

was introduced in the United States in 1911. Group credit insurance was introduced in 1926. There were various attempts to introduce life insurance on a group basis in the nineteenth century, notably by fraternal societies in the United States and friendly societies in the United Kingdom, using the 'assessment' principle, whereby each member pays the same contribution irrespective of age. These ran into difficulties apparently because of optional membership and lack of an age limitation rule, resulting in severe problems between generations. The existence of an age limit implies that there should be some provision for the ex-members over the age limit. For this reason, the growth of group life insurance for employees has been associated with the growth of pension schemes, which often provide death-in-service benefits for the members without the use of a group life insurance scheme as described above. However, in the United States the tax regulations have favoured the growth of group life insurance as opposed to death-in-service benefits for occupational pension schemes.[1]

The provision of life insurance on a group basis can be described as a world-wide twentieth-century trend

[1]McGill (1964) summarises the difference in the tax treatment of the benefits received as follows (p. 98): 'Many employers prefer to provide death benefits under a group life insurance program rather than under a pension plan. Among the motivating factors is that group life insurance proceeds are completely exempt from federal income taxation, whereas lump sum distributions from a pension plan in excess of $5000 are subject to income taxation on a capital gains basis. On the other hand, group life insurance proceeds are includible in the gross estate of the decedent for estate tax purposes, while under a qualified pension plan death benefits attributable to employers' contributions are excludible from the gross estate when paid to a designated beneficiary.'

through the growth of employee benefit schemes and state social security. We are specifically interested in group life insurance of the yearly renewable kind. This is important in Canada, France, Sweden and the United States[1] but it is not so important in West Germany, the Netherlands and the United Kingdom. The relative importance of this business as a percentage of all life insurance business is shown in table III for the former group of countries. It can be seen that group life insurance has been of growing importance in the former countries.

TABLE III

THE PERCENTAGE OF LIFE INSURANCE IN FORCE WHICH IS PROVIDED BY GROUP LIFE SCHEMES, IN FOUR COUNTRIES: 1950, 1960 AND 1969

	1950	*1960*	*1969*
Canada	16·4	31·4	46·0
France	34·2	53·4	60·2
Sweden	1·7	16·2	70·3
United States	20·4	27·9	37·6

Table IV shows the statistics, life insurance in force/the total assets of life insurance companies, for seven countries. It can be seen that in 1972 the ratio was substantially higher in Canada, France, Sweden and the United States than in Germany, The Netherlands and the United Kingdom and was particularly high in France and Sweden as a result of the high

[1]Whether or not group life insurance is of the yearly renewable kind is not generally specified in the statistical literature but the ratio, life insurance in force/annual premium payments can be calculated for group life business and if this is roughly 100 or more then it can be assumed that most of the cover is indeed renewable every year.

proportion of group life business in these two countries. The growth of the ratios in the first four countries also reflects the growth of group life business.

TABLE IV

THE RATIO: ALL LIFE INSURANCE IN FORCE/TOTAL ASSETS OF LIFE INSURANCE COMPANIES, IN SEVEN COUNTRIES: 1950, 1960 and 1972

	1950	*1960*	*1972*
Canada	3·5	4·8	7·9
France	7·4*	8·9	17·2
Sweden	4·3*	6·7	9·5
United States	3·9	5·2	7·3
Germany	5·6	4·6	4·8
Netherlands	4·3*	4·7	5·6
United Kingdom	3·3*	3·4	3·1

*1955

An essential feature of group life insurance is that it is provided without individual medical check-ups or evidence of insurability.[1] The character of the group may be taken into account in calculating premium charges; there will be a difference, for example, between a group of miners and a group of vicars, but individual risks are not recorded. In contrast, individual policies require declarations of good health and details relating to impairments or possible impairments; medical examinations are also often required. Owing to these health considerations individual life insurance is hardly ever written on a yearly renewable basis. First, if declarations of good health or medical check-ups are required each year

[1]For smaller schemes evidence of insurability is sometimes required for new entrants.

then, should the policy-holder become ill, he may not be able to renew his cover; and second, if medical check-ups are not required, then the insurance company may become subject to 'adverse selection', that is the insurance company may be left with the poorer risks as the fitter policy-holders will not renew their policies if they can obtain cheaper cover elsewhere.[1] Premium charges can be increased to compensate for adverse selection, but this tends to discourage the good risks, who can get cheaper cover elsewhere. These difficulties are avoided if the individual policy is not on a yearly renewable basis and both the sum insured and the premium payments are determined before the commencement of the policy by criteria other than changes in health. The insurance company then cannot increase the premium charge if the policy-holder becomes ill, and the policy-holder cannot discontinue the policy if he remains well, at least without compensating the insurance company by paying a surrender charge. The need for the payment of a surrender charge implies that the policy should have a saving component

There is an incentive for life insurance companies to maximise the amount of premium income rather than the insurance cover. This is a further reason for a saving component in individual policies. Term insurance policies are not very good business unless they are for very large amounts. 'Convertible' term insurance policies are sold in the United States in the hope that they will later be converted into whole life policies.

[1]There seems to be actually little or no published evidence that those who discontinue their life policies have better health than those who continue, Institute of Life Insurance (1941), p. 42.

On the other hand group life insurance schemes written on a yearly renewable basis contain virtually no savings component. Even the simplest individual term insurance policy, with level premiums and sum insured, contains a saving component since part of the initial premiums have to contribute towards the increased probability of dying later on. As the term of the policy increases it turns into a whole life policy which has a considerable saving component. This elongation process began in Great Britain in the early nineteenth century with the growth of whole life business, when the earliest policies were term insurance. The lack of saving component in group life schemes means that they are unaffected by inflation, so that high rates of inflation promote the growth of group schemes. In Brazil, for example, practically all life insurance in force is provided by group schemes.

In order to calculate the premiums for an individual life insurance policy it is necessary to have a mortality table. Mortality tables are generally prescribed or have to be approved by government control authorities. The chief concern of the authorities is to ensure solvency. For this reason, and also for reasons of prudent commercial practice, the mortality tables used for calculating the premiums of individual life insurance policies tend to over-estimate the mortality probabilities. They do this by containing an explicit safety margin or by being out-of-date so that recent declines in mortality rates are not taken into account. The tables used for annuities conversely tend to under-estimate the mortality rates.

Group schemes reduce the importance of mortality tables in the calculation of premiums. For large schemes containing thousands of people a very approximate knowledge of ages is adequate. It can suffice to know that the group is not noticeably ageing and that there are a reasonable number of new entrants in the lower age groups. As the size of the group increases the previous claims experience becomes more important than mortality assumptions based on mortality tables.[1] The risk element of the scheme decreases with increasing size so that for a scheme with as many as fifty or one hundred thousand members the premiums can be determined by the claims experience to such an extent that the scheme is on a self financing basis, the premiums exactly paying for the claims as they arise. The larger a scheme is, the more accurately the return obtained from contributions and the charges of the insurer can be assessed. Insurance is a mirror image to personal saving in this respect, because the visibility to the saver of the expense charges in a saving media improves the less the rate of return to different savers is interdependent. The moral is that in insurance there is safety in large groups whereas in saving, reliance on others should be treated with caution.

The subject of mortality tables is rather sensitive because it cannot be separated from the subject of the expense charges of the insurance company. It is not really possible to provide a satisfactory separation of the expense component and the genuine risk component of an individually purchased life insurance policy. The concept of a mortality probability is itself subjective as it depends on an endless number of

[1]Insurers like to calculate premiums using conservative assumptions and then return an excess charge as a bonus. The subject of how to calculate bonuses from previous claims experience is known as 'credibility theory'. See Beard *et al.* (1969).

factors such as: the policy-holder's occupation, where he lives, how many cigarettes he smokes each day, whether he is married, how much driving he does. The more that is known about the policy-holder the more accurately the mortality probability can be determined. Furthermore, the mortality experience of different companies varies considerably so that it is legitimate for them to charge different rates.

The administrative expenses of a group life insurance scheme are much less than those of a collection of individual policies providing the same cover. The operating expenses of life companies are usually about 20 per cent of the premium receipts. Of these expenses about 40 per cent go in selling costs. The operating expenses of group life policies are generally less than half this amount as a percentage of premium receipts and therefore as a percentage of the sum insured is very much smaller.[1] Selling costs are very much less for group life policies than for individual policies.

The individual life insurance policy provides a degree of personal choice of insurance cover which the group policy cannot provide. However, because individual policies are not written on a yearly renewable basis they contain a kind of inflexibility in the year to year insurance cover which group policies do not contain. The amount of life insurance cover provided by group policies can be linked automatically to family responsibilities and salary levels, but

[1]An international comparative study of operating expenses is contained in *Eurofinance* (1971), p. 92. According to the *Life Insurance Fact Book* (1973), p. 64, in the United States the operating expenses as a percentage of premium and investment income in 1972 are 17 per cent of all business, which includes 7·2 per cent which was commission to brokers. For ordinary business this expense ratio was 19·8 per cent and for group business it was 9·3 per cent.

if the individual policy-holder wants to increase his insurance cover, unless suitable options are available under his policy, he has to take out a new one. In this way he may collect several policies so that the total insurance cover is provided in layers. This layering effect is intrinsic to individual life insurance.

The introduction of an insurance component into a saving scheme tends to have a blurring effect on the visibility of the expense charges. For example, in the United Kingdom the expenses of unit trusts are controlled, that is subject to legal maxima. However, the expenses of unit-linked life assurance are not controlled. Under these policies a proportion of the premium is generally subtracted and the remainder invested in units, income from the units being re-invested in further units. The proportion subtracted for an endowment policy running from 25–40 years of age is approximately 5 per cent. but many policies charge appreciably more. The sum assured receivable on death for such a policy is typically fifteen times the annual premium payments or the bid value of the units allocated whichever is greater. There may be no guaranteed minimum sum provided when the policy matures at 40 years of age. The 5 per cent charge is in fact expensive if this is just for insurance cover. A report of a government committee in the United Kingdom on linked life assurance makes the following comments on expense charges:[1]

> Many of our witnesses referred to the possibility of introducing some control over the charging structure of policies. . . . This question is often seen as the counterpart of the control exercised over the

[1]*Scott Report* (1973), p. 47.

service charge levied by the managers of authorised unit trusts. We think this oversimplifies the issue. In the case of the authorised unit trust, the service charges are required essentially to defray selling costs and the costs of managing the investors' funds. In the case of a typical linked policy there are also minimum benefit guarantees for which provision must be made, the cost of which varies between policy-holders.

In nearly all European countries it is possible to pay life assurance premiums to some extent before tax. This is not possible however in the United States. In the United Kingdom this tax concession is equal to 17·5 per cent of the premium.[1] This is usually worth more than the total insurance component of the policy. For example, under the fifteen-year unit-linked endowment policy, with 5 per cent of the premium subtracted each year to pay for the insurance cover, the insurance component of the policy is worth only 5 per cent of the premium. An employer pays the premium of a group life insurance policy before tax but this concession is worth less than the cost of the insurance cover. In this sense tax incentives are weighted in favour of individual rather than group life insurance. In the author's opinion this weighting cannot be justified.

Group life insurance schemes are a more efficient and cheaper way of providing life insurance cover than individual policies. But the latter also have a substantial saving component. However, the interaction of the insurance component of life assurance policies

[1]Under the 'unified' system of income tax introduced in 1973, for premiums over £20 per annum.

with the savings component produces various distorting effects which tend to detract from the value of the life assurance policy as a saving scheme. This value is determined by such things as: surrender values, paid-up values, the variability of premium payments, the visibility of expense charges and the visibility of the rates of return. The existence of the insurance component combined with the saving component in the life assurance policy greatly complicates these factors, and therefore puts the saver at a disadvantage vis-à-vis the insurance company's experts.

A change in the regulations in the United Kingdom is suggested so that life assurance policies need no longer contain an insurance component in order to qualify for a tax concession for the premium payments. This suggestion is discussed further in chapter 4. Of course, if the insurance component is removed from a life assurance policy it becomes just a saving scheme. Under the suggested change the existence of an insurance component will be optional. The possible resulting loss of individual life insurance cover can be compensated for by a strengthening of life insurance provided on a group basis. In particular, mortgage protection life insurance could be compulsory and provided by group schemes.

About 85 per cent of credit life insurance in the United States is provided by group schemes. However, there are few group credit schemes in the United Kingdom and, in particular, there do not appear to be any group mortgage protection policies. Group credit insurance as practised in the United States is a very pure kind of group insurance. All the schemes are large and coverage is nearly always automatic or compulsory. Credit worthiness tends to be related to insurability so that evidence of insurability is hardly ever asked for. Mortgage holders, particularly, tend to be reasonably young, fit and working and as they grow older their mortgage liability tends to decline, so they form an eminently insurable group. Details of ages are seldom taken (subject to the usual age limitation). A charge for the cover is generally made by a small increase to the rate of interest.

There is considerable scope for the introduction of group mortgage protection schemes into the United Kingdom. At the present time mortgage protection for building society mortgages is provided by individual policies which are either purchased through the local branches or by the borrower himself dealing directly with an insurance company. Local branches often have lists of insurance companies which they use or recommend for mortgage protection according to a rota system.

About 15 per cent of mortgages in the United Kingdom are repaid under 'endowment plan' schemes. Under this system mortgage holders do not make regular capital repayments each year, but take on an endowment policy instead which is earmarked to pay back all of the mortgage capital when it matures. If, as suggested, the same tax concessions were provided in the United Kingdom for saving schemes as are provided for endowment policies, then it would be possible to have endowment plans with the insurance provided by a group mortgage protection policy, and the mortgage capital repayment ensured by a saving scheme. Therefore, the suggested change would tend to encourage the growth of group mortgage protection policies. Group policies are more difficult to introduce if some people are being covered separately through endowment policies.

Which particular groups in society should insure themselves is a question fundamental to the whole area of insurance, including health and disability insurance. The provision of widows' benefits on a national basis by means of state social security has intrinsically different characteristics from the provision of widows' benefits for employee groups. In particular it is difficult on a national basis to link death benefits to pay. Governments generally encourage life insurance cover on an individual basis by means of tax concessions and on a national basis by means of state social security, but it is important not to neglect the intermediate groups between the single individual and that which is the whole of society.

The growth of the provision of life insurance on a group basis has promoted a separation of life insurance from personal saving. This trend has been most beneficial for savers as it allows them to direct saving from life assurance policies to other means of saving, thus permitting a greater freedom of choice.

CHAPTER 3

The Visibility of the Cost of the Benefits and the Rate of Return provided by Life Assurance and Annuity Policies

To the extent that a life assurance policy is a saving scheme a knowledge of the rate of return it provides is desirable as a standard of comparison with other means of saving. However, the concept of a rate of return is not appropriate for term insurance policies and related policies where the insurance component of the policy predominates over the saving component. In the case of the linked life assurance policies it is possible to separate the insurance component from the savings component of the policy so one can evaluate the rate of return from the saving component and cost of the insurance component separately. In the case of traditional life assurance policies, either a rate of return can be calculated and a mortality rate assumed or a measure of the cost of the insurance cover can be calculated with an assumption about the rate of return obtained from the saving component of the policy.

In the United States, under the influence of 'consumerism', there has been a considerable amount of research into methods of measuring the cost of the life insurance cover provided by different policies. Several different indices of cost have been developed,[1]

[1]A description of different indices is contained in the Institute of Life Assurance (1970).

the purpose of which is to reduce the considerable complexity of life assurance policies in the United States to a single figure, thus making possible the comparison of the costs of different policies. Recently, there has been a movement towards making 'price disclosure' based on a 'cost index' compulsory, one of the foremost campaigners being Professor J. M. Belth who advocated that regulatory authorities should concern themselves with this subject; he stated that:[1]

> the enormous complexity of the life insurance policy contract places even the reasonably intelligent buyer at a disadvantage in his relations with an insurance company, and it would seem to be an appropriate regulatory function to correct this imbalance between buyer and seller . . . and, if price disclosure is the most preferable alternative to the *status quo*, is meaningful price disclosure in life insurance feasible? It is possible to say no on the grounds that price analysis of a life insurance policy is a problem sufficiently complex to preclude meaningful disclosure. In the author's opinion, however, meaningful price disclosure in life insurance is definitely feasible.

The National Association of Insurance Commissioners has developed model regulations for price disclosure using the 'interest-adjusted index',[2] and

[1]Belth (1966), p. 245.

[2]The interest-adjusted ten-year index is, per $1000 initial face value (sum assured) the discounted future ten-year premium payments less the discounted bonuses for ten years, less the discounted surrender value of the policy at the end of ten years. This is all divided by a scaling factor (less than ten) which

under these regulations potential policy-holders would be able to obtain the value of this index on request.

In order to see clearly the rate of return provided by a savings scheme the savings must accumulate either in an account like a bank account to which interest is credited or in an account of the shares of an investment fund which have a known capital value and dividend receipts. However, traditional life assurance policies are different. Under a whole life policy a guaranteed 'sum assured' is paid in the event of death whenever it occurs, and under an endowment policy, the sum assured is paid at a certain date or in the event of death before this date. Various bonuses, which are calculated and paid in numerous ways throughout the world, may be provided. These traditional policies are, however, otherwise surprisingly similar in design.

In the author's opinion the concept of the rate of return obtained from an endowment or whole life policy is more helpful than a cost index giving cost per \$1000 face value (sum assured). A cost index has to assume a rate of interest, the choice of which will greatly effect the result according to the number of years that are taken into account when calculating the index, whereas the calculation of a rate of return is not so highly dependent on a mortality assumption.[1]

---

represents the fact that a ten-year term was taken but that the value of the \$1000 depreciated with time. A 20-year index is defined similarly.

[1]Consider the following calculation: fixed unit sum assured is discounted at x per cent per annum until the death of the policy-holder. This discounted value is approximately $(1+x/100)^{-n}$, where n is the expectation of life of the policy-holder. This is approximately $\exp(-x \times n/100)$ which is a function of $x \times n$. The value of n only varies by a small amount according to the mortality table used to calculate it.

The calculation of either a rate of return or a sophisticated cost index is a complicated procedure best left to a computer. The whole area is rather problematical, one reason being that the need for a cost index depends on the extent to which past performance or specimen bonus rates are a guide to future performance.

The calculation of the rate of return of a cost index is further complicated by taking into account that policies often do not run their full course.[1] If a traditional policy is surrendered in the first three years, only at most a low proportion of the premium payments are returned. In the United Kingdom the surrender value of participating and non-participating policies are generally the same for particular companies per £1000 initial sum assured. In addition, participating policies receive the surrender value of declared reversionary bonuses and, although this may be quite generous[2] the terminal bonus is generally lost, and this makes the cashing-in of bonuses disadvantageous. In the United Kingdom terminal bonuses can be quite substantial and are provided by nearly all companies as a maturity or death benefit, but are not provided for surrenders. They are also quite common in the United States, though not to the same extent as in the United Kingdom, and companies

[1]Belth (1966) and (1968).

[2]There is a difference according to whether it is simple interest or compound interest reversionary bonus. In the case of the simple interest bonus the terminal bonus is generally calculated as a percentage of the reversionary bonus, so that the cashing-in of the reversionary bonus results in the future loss of terminal bonus. The surrender value of a compound interest reversionary bonus tends to be unfavourable because the interest is then paid on a reduced sum assured.

in the United States provide 'terminal dividends' for surrenders.[1]

The superior investment performance of shares compared with fixed interest securities over considerable periods of time, has promoted the development of new kinds of life assurance policy the designs of which permit the benefits to be based on investments in shares.[2] These policies are of two types. The first is akin to a saving scheme with an attached insurance component. The premiums accumulate in an account such as a bank account or an account of units of a unit trust, with additional specified charges to pay for the insurance component of the policy. The balance of the account and the income from it, which is then invested in that account, are known to the policyholder. In the United Kingdom 'linked life assurance' policies are of this type.[3]

The second type of policies, which do not exist in the United Kingdom, resemble the designs of traditional policies, but with modifications to allow the benefits both to increase and decrease according to investment results. Perhaps the simplest of these designs to understand is the 'Dutch' design, introduced into Holland in 1956, which is like that of a traditional policy except that everything, that is the premiums,

[1]The word 'dividend' in the USA corresponds to 'bonus' in the UK. Under New York State law if a terminal dividend is provided, then policies terminating due to surrender must not be exempted. The regular payment of terminal bonuses was introduced in 1915 by the Metropolitan Life Insurance Company.

[2]A description of such policies in many countries, including the New York Life design, is contained in 19th *International Congress of Actuaries* (1972), Vol. I.

[3]With a very few exceptions. For example there are some hybrid policies in which the investment income from the linked life policy is used to purchase traditionally defined benefits.

sum assured and surrender values are all expressed in terms of units instead of amounts of money.[1] The capital value of these policies depends directly on the investment performance of an investment fund or unit trust. This type of policy is known as 'variable life insurance' and will be introduced soon in the United States.

The difference between these two kinds of policy is, in fact, a question of presentation. This will be demonstrated in the case of the 'New York Life design' of variable life insurance policy in the United States (see page 59). The second type of design has no merits for policy-holders compared to designs which have a well-defined and clearly visible savings component. They are greatly inferior with respect to visibility of the rate of return provided, the charges for the insurance component and expenses, and the method of calculating surrender values.

The insurance component of a policy of the first type is the amount payable on death less the accumulated savings in the account. This is known as the 'sum at risk'. From the point of view of the protection of the policy-holder, the deductions to be made to pay for the insurance component and also the expense charges should be pre-determined before the commencement of the policy and supplied to the policy-holder. Most linked life assurance policies in the United Kingdom seek to do this. In order to pre-determine the charges for the insurance component based on mortality assumptions only, there must be

[1]The units vary by a factor of $(1+x/100)/(1+i/100)$ on valuation dates where x per cent is the investment earnings including income and capital gains since the last valuation date, and i per cent is the investment return assumption (IRA) assumed in the model.

frequent charges to pay for the insurance risk over short periods of time, otherwise assumptions about investment earnings have to be made. In addition, the ratio: sum at risk/corresponding charge, must not depend on investment performance. This implies that if the pre-determined charge for the insurance component is defined as a percentage of the premiums, then the sum at risk must be a multiple of the premiums. Similarly, if the charges for the insurance component come from percentage deductions from the savings capital then the sum at risk must be a multiple of this capital.

The most common kind of level premium linked life assurance policy in the United Kingdom has small deductions from the premiums to pay for the insurance component.[1] Single premium policies generally have a sum assured which is a multiple of the accumulated saving capital and this is paid for by a pre-determined percentage deduction from this capital. One company is very successfully selling a level premium whole life policy[2] for which the sum assured is a multiple of the accumulated savings capital (after an initial 'guarantee period').

Table V shows examples of the percentages used to define these three kinds of policy. In the first of the specimen policies the death benefit is fixed by a simple formula and the corresponding charge for the insur-

[1]These generally have a death benefit which is either the accumulated saving or a fixed sum assured, whichever is the greater. The sum at risk in this case actually depends on the investment performance of the fund whereas the deductions are fixed. This scarcely presents problems in practice since the deductions tend to be small and the corresponding sums at risk to be large compared to the annual premium payments.

[2]The premium is £6·55 per initial £1000 sum assured at 23 years of age, £9·58 at 32, £12·27 at 38, and £23·14 at 50.

TABLE V

THE PERCENTAGES USED TO DEFINE THREE KINDS OF LINKED LIFE ASSURANCE POLICY

Type of policy	1 Qualifying level premium endowment policy (taken out at age 30)	2 Single premium policy (taken out at any age)	3 Level premium whole life policy (taken out at age 24)
Type of percentage Age of policy-holder	The percentage deduction from the premiums to pay for the life insurance cover.	The percentage multiple of the saving payable on death.	The percentage multiple of the saving payable on death.
30	20·8 (for first year only)	250	(guarantee period)
35	5	232	
40	5	190	1020
45	5	157	636
50	3	130	444
55	3	118	330
60	3	111	260
65	3	106	210
70	3	104	178
75	3	102	154
80	3	101	135
Death benefit or charge for the insurance cover.	The amount payable on death is 180 times the monthly premium or the value of the saving, whichever is the greater.	There is an annual charge of $\frac{1}{2}$ per cent of the saving capital.	The charge for the insurance cover is not pre-determined.

ance cover by a table of figures. Conversely, in the second of the specimen policies the charge for the insurance cover is fixed by a simple formula and the death benefit is defined by a table of figures. The third policy also has a death benefit, defined by a table of figures which are multiples of the accumulated savings capital. However, for this latter policy it is not possible to define the charge for the insurance cover by a simple percentage of the accumulated savings, because this is a level premium policy and a constant percentage charge would result in the insurance cover changing in an unsatisfactory way. In order to pre-determine the charge for the insurance cover for this third policy, it is necessary to have another table of figures showing this charge as a percentage of the accumulated savings for each year of the policy.

For several years there has been a debate in the United States about the introduction of 'variable life insurance'. Several different designs have been developed of which the New York Life design and the Walker design may be introduced in the near future.[1] In these two designs, as for traditional policies, a basic role is played by the assumption concerning future investment performance. This is known as the 'investment return assumption' (IRA). Different designs of variable life insurance policy correspond to different methods of allocating the 'excess interest' earnings arising from the difference between the actual return obtained and the IRA.

The New York Life design is actually very similar to the third design of linked life assurance policy mentioned above, and works in the following way.

[1]Leckie (1972).

Suppose that the accumulated savings for the linked life policy are called the 'reserves', then the ratio of the sum assured to the reserves is pre-determined for both policies and does not depend on investment performance. For the linked life policy, as for the variable life design, an IRA is defined, and the sum assured is determined for both policies in such a fashion that if the investment performance exactly equals the IRA then the sum assured is constant. Thus the New York Life design can be defined for policy-holders by three tables showing: pre-determined ratios of the sum assured to the reserves for each year of the policy; pre-determined charges for the insurance cover expressed as percentages of the reserves; and pre-determined surrender charges (that is the differences between the surrender values and the reserves, expressed as percentages of the reserves). Also the expense charges could be stated on policies and the value of the reserves given to policy-holders each year instead of only the sum assured and surrender value. In this way the charges for the insurance and expenses, and also the return from the savings component of the policy would be fully visible.

In the United States the business for endowment policies is relatively small compared to that for whole life policies. The designs of variable life policies which have been developed in the United States are whole life policies. The insurance component of these proposed variable life policies will therefore be quite large. Furthermore regulations have been developed which specify the minimum sum payable in the event of death in terms of a multiple of the annual premium payments. The multiple, which is dependent on the age at which the policy was taken out, is illustrated in table VI.

TABLE VI

THE MINIMUM DEATH BENEFIT TO BE PROVIDED BY VARIABLE LIFE INSURANCE POLICIES IN THE UNITED STATES[1]

Issue ages	*The multiples of the annual premium to be paid in the event of death*
0–5	80
6–10	71
11–15	63
16–20	55
21–25	47
26–30	40
31–35	33
36–40	27
41–45	21
46–50	15
51–55	13
56–60	11
61–65	9
66–70	8
71 and over	7

Further the policy must provide coverage for the whole life for an amount not less than the initial stated amount. It can be seen that these rules are designed for level premium whole life policies.

Although the United States does not yet have linked or variable life policies, it was probably the first country to have variable annuities. These were first introduced by the Teachers' Insurance and Annuity Association for college staff in 1952. Under a variable deferred annuity, units of an investment fund are accumulated before retirement, income from the

[1]Rule 3c–4, Investment Company Act. This rule was developed by the Securities and Exchange Commission.

units being invested in further units. Variable deferred annuity policies present the possibility of a low pension because retirement occurs when market values are low, and therefore might be thought to be unduly risky compared to traditional policies. If at the moment of retirement the accumulated units have to be cashed in and a fixed pension purchased, then clearly market values at the time are important. However, if the pension is itself variable then these market values are not so important.

There are two general designs of variable annuity policy corresponding to two different methods of defining the pension from the performance of the annuity fund. The difference between these designs is analogous to the difference between the design of linked life policies in the United Kingdom and the variable life policies in the United States discussed earlier in this chapter. The second design resembles that of traditional annuity policies and the IRA is a basic feature.

Under the first design units are not cashed in on retirement but retained. Each pensioner then receives the yearly income I from his units plus a small percentage of their capital value V, so that his yearly pension may be expressed by the formula $I+kV$. The kV component can be seen as arising from selling the units of those who die and distributing the proceeds amongst the living pensioners. k is an actuarial quantity dependent on mortality and cost experience and expectations, and independent of investment experience or expectations. It is approximately the reciprocal of the expectation of life on retirement less an amount for costs. k, which is about 0·06, can either be the same for all male or female pensioners who retired at the same age, and varied slightly from time to time, or can be fixed for all pensioners of the same sex retiring at the same age in the same year, remain fixed for each pensioner but vary from time to time for new entrants.

The large income component in the pension of the first design produces a quite smoothly varying pension. The dividend receipts from a group of shares do not vary greatly from year to year whereas their market price is subject to considerable fluctuations.[1]

This design does not appear to be used at all in the United States, and is only used to a relatively small extent in the United Kingdom compared to the second design. Some companies in the United Kingdom provide a variable annuity using this design linked to unit trust units. However only a proportion of the income from the units is provided as a pension, so that the pension is determined by the formula k_1I+k_2V. In one particular example the pension is paid quarterly. The value of I is the previous year's income and V is the current capital value. For a man retiring at age 65, $k_1=63$ per cent, $k_2=1{\cdot}747$ per cent for the quarterly payment which is equivalent to $k_1=0{\cdot}63$ and $k_2=\frac{1{\cdot}747}{100}\times 4=0{\cdot}070$ if payments were made yearly. There is a guarantee

[1]The standard deviation of the annual percentage change of share prices in the United Kingdom from 1919–1971 calculated from the share index of De Zoete and Bevan (1972) is 19·4 per cent. The corresponding figure for the dividend income derived from a lump sum investment in the index in 1919 is 9·4 per cent. Turner (1970) calculates the standard deviation of the annual change of Standard and Poor's Composite Share Index over the period 1880–1967 to be 20·3 per cent and over the period 1946–67 to be 14·77 per cent.

that for a particular policy the annuity payments will not fall below the rate provided at the start of the policy. When this guarantee is exercised it is paid for by reductions in the payments in subsequent years.

The second design is less satisfactory than the first from the point of view of the comprehensibility of the method of calculating benefits as pensioners cannot be expected to understand the valuation procedure on which this design is based. The rate of pension payments is adjusted at yearly or more frequent valuation dates. An actuarial liability for each pension is calculated, by assuming that current rates will be maintained and then discounting the value of the future payments according to an investment return assumption and a mortality and cost assumption.[1] The rate of pension payments is then adjusted by the same proportion until the total of all the actuarial liabilities equals the capital value of the 'annuity fund' supporting the pensions. The initial pension provided on retirement is calculated so that its actuarial liability is equal to the sum used to purchase it. For a variable deferred annuity this is the final capital value of the units accumulated before retirement.

For a variable deferred annuity providing a pension calculated according to the second design the assets of the annuity fund supporting the pension can be the same as those supporting the units accumulated before retirement. This means that if retirement takes place when the market value of the investments are

[1]If p(x) is the probability of a particular pensioner being alive in x years' time, where p(o) = 1; then the actuarial liability resulting from future yearly payments of £k to this pensioner while he lives, starting now, is £k $\sum_{x=0}$ p(x)(1 + i/100)$^{-x}$, cent is the IRA.

particularly low then the initial pension will be correspondingly low but will rise later as prices recover. The change in the pension from year to year is almost entirely determined by the investment performance of the assets during the year. It is the return from the assets including both income and capital gains minus the IRA.[1] This results in a pension which fluctuates from year to year more than that produced by the first design. The larger the IRA, the bigger the initial pension but the more slowly it increases from year to year. IRAs of about 4 and $3\frac{1}{2}$ per cent are typical. IRAs with these values tend to produce pensions increasing more rapidly than those produced by the first design.

An account providing a fixed guaranteed rate of interest will produce a guaranteed lump sum at a future date in return for particular contributions. Obviously, a guaranteed rate of interest plus a bonus additional rate of interest will produce a guaranteed lump sum at a future date plus a bonus addition. Therefore, the specification of a lump sum benefit at a future date in return for particular contributions, whether under an endowment policy or a deferred annuity, instead of the provision of an account with a guaranteed rate of interest, is to a considerable extent just a question of presentation. The provision of an account has the advantage that the rate of return provided for the accumulated contributions and their present value is clearly visible.

Life insurance companies actually do provide interest-bearing accounts. The kind of insured pension

[1]More precisely, assuming expense and mortality assumptions are realised, it changes by the same factor as that given for the units of the Dutch design in footnote 1 on page 55.

scheme known as 'deposit administration' is based on the accumulation of money in an interest-bearing account from which pensions are purchased for members of the scheme as they retire. In the United States this kind of scheme widely replaced the 'group deferred annuity', and they in turn are being replaced by schemes based on separate accounts. The reserves for these kinds of schemes are shown in diagram 9. Under the group deferred annuity scheme a specified amount of future pension is bought for each member. The calculation of the overall rate of return obtained from a large number of deferred annuities may not be possible in practice. The greater simplicity of deposit administration for the larger insured pension schemes compared with group deferred annuities, the improved visibility of present values and the rate of return provided account for it largely replacing group deferred annuity schemes in the United States.

In the United Kingdom there are not many deposit administration schemes, but a variety of insured pension schemes known as 'controlled funding' has become important. The pension provided by these schemes is generally based on final salary, and the contribution required from the employer to fund the scheme is calculated each year by the insurance company, using a group deferred annuity principle. Owing to the nature of the reversionary and terminal bonus system this calculation is complicated.[1]

[1]A critique of these schemes by Norman Freethy in *Handbook on Pensions and Employee Benefits* states that there is a tendency to keep initial contributions low in order to sell the scheme, pp. 6.2–09: 'insurance companies employ sometimes quite sophisticated techniques to keep the initial contributions rate as low as possible. Indeed some of the bases adopted by insurance companies for "controlled funding" are so sophisticated as to be almost totally obscure. In these circumstances it is virtually impossible to ascertain what a scheme is really going to cost.'

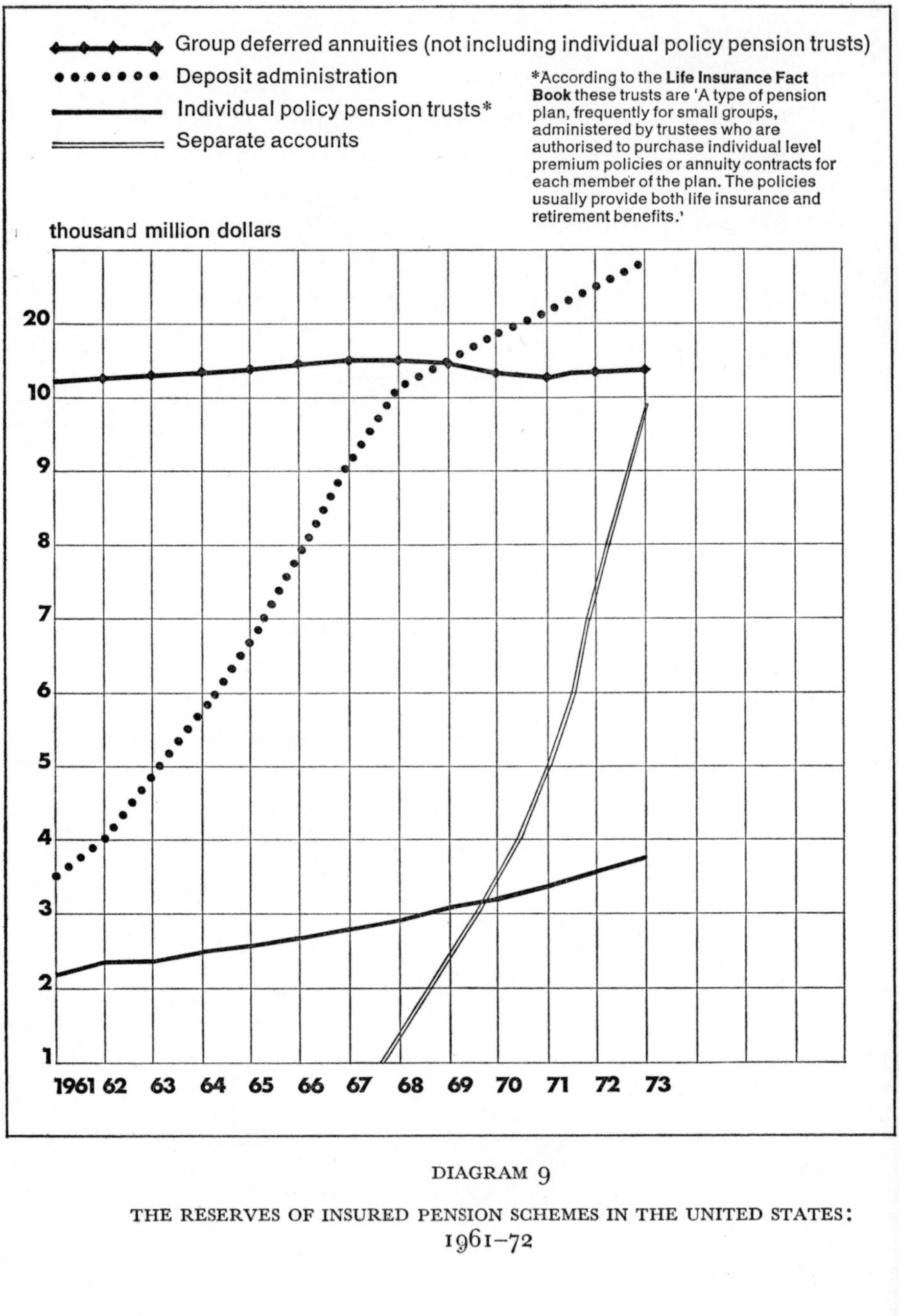

DIAGRAM 9

THE RESERVES OF INSURED PENSION SCHEMES IN THE UNITED STATES: 1961–72

An interesting discussion about insured pension schemes in the United Kingdom followed the recent paper by Fellows (1972), in which the visibility of rates of return was discussed. One contributor recommended that life insurance companies should provide a deposit administration or managed fund facility on the grounds that in this respect they are superior to group deferred annuities:[1]

> It is extremely difficult to establish just what the total investment yield is on a group deferred annuity policy. . . . The total yield on a pension fund's investments is such an important factor, and there is so much at stake, that it cannot be surprising if questions as to yield are increasingly asked. I would go so far as to suggest that any office which considers itself to be in pensions business to a significant extent should, if it has not done so already, make available as soon as possible either a managed fund facility or a deposit administration contract or both. To put it at its lowest the availability of such contracts would prevent the understandable presumption which is increasingly made in financial matters: namely, that non-disclosure of what seems to be reasonable information might be taken as evidence that there is something to hide.

For traditional group and individually purchased deferred annuity schemes in the United States and United Kingdom a distinction can be made between those using 'single premium funding' and those using

[1]Fellows (1972), p. 58.

'level premium funding'. Single premium funding essentially consists of a succession of single premium policies, one for each year's contribution, each providing a particular lump sum on retirement or pension equivalent to which bonuses may be added. Information about the benefits bought for each year's contribution is presented in table form. Under level premium funding (sometimes known as 'annual premium funding' in the United Kingdom) the future benefit is defined only in return for regular equal contributions until retirement. Single premium funding permits a more natural flexibility of contributions than level premium funding. If the contributions decrease under a scheme using level premium funding, then the future guaranteed benefits have to be decreased. Under the reversionary and terminal bonus system in the United Kingdom the technical character of this calculation puts the policy-holder at a disadvantage should he query the results of the actuary's computations. There is a trend towards single premium funding for traditional deferred annuity policies in the United Kingdom, but a large proportion of those on sale still use level premium funding even where flexibility of contributions is stressed. There is only a small amount of business for traditional deferred annuity policies in the United States.

Group deferred annuity schemes in the United States virtually all use single premium funding with the exception of individual policy pension trusts (see diagram 8). In the United Kingdom, however, many of these schemes use level premium funding. Under the author's own pension scheme,[1] for example, whenever there is a pay increase members have to

[1]Federated Superannuation System for Universities.

choose a new level premium policy from over one hundred different options, while continuing to maintain the old policies. In this way members accumulate many different policies. So that this scheme is most cumbersome to administer.

The accumulation of money in an account under a deposit administration contract does not imply that it is possible for an employer to withdraw the money in the account on request. A study of the transferability of deposit administration and group deferred annuity schemes was made by the *Institutional Investor Study Report*. This study begins with the following passage:[1]

> If a pension-benefit plan is funded in a bank managed trust account, a bank managing agency account, a bank comingled employee-benefit-plan account, or in an individual account managed by an investment counselling firm, or in a mutual fund, the plan's interest in any of these investment accounts can normally be expeditiously redeemed or transferred to another managing trustee or agent. The transfer of interests in an insurance company's account to another funding agent has historically been a more complex task. Many employers, upon investigating the possibility of shifting funds to another manager, have found (1) that their contract prohibits such action, or (2) a transfer can be effected, but a substantial surrender charge is incurred and/or the insurer reserves the right to stretch the payout over a long period of time, perhaps ten years or more.

The primary reason for the difficulties involved in

[1]Securities and Exchange Commission (1971), Vol. II, p. 577.

immediate withdrawal of money from a deposit administration account is that the fixed interest investments covering the account have depreciated in capital value due to rising interest rates, illustrated in diagram 10. In the United Kingdom there is sometimes a considerable difference between the closure values to insured pension schemes according to whether or not the money is being invested in a managed fund of the same insurance company.[1] The general effect of the loss of business on the profits or surplus of the company therefore also has an influence on closure values.

Do traditional life assurance policies have any merits for policy-holders compared to linked life assurance policies? The guaranteeing of a fixed sum assured in return for fixed premium payments is a simple and good design for term insurance policies, but for whole life and endowment policies complications inevitably occur with the payment of bonuses and surrender values. Policy-holders have a legal right to participate in profits in many countries.[2] Lack of participation in profits by holders of without-profit policies in the United Kingdom has caused some misgivings within the insurance industry during the

[1]Fellows (1972): 'some of the differentials in closure values apparently being quoted by life offices, depending on whether or not the cash sum involved was going into that particular company's managed fund, were quite enormous. It was not unknown in his experience to find the larger of the two values was something like two and a half times the smaller one' (p. 58).

[2]In general, participating policies only are permitted in Belgium, Finland, France, Germany, Norway, Sweden, and in the United States for mutual companies under New York State legislation. There are some minor exceptions including term insurance, but not conventional endowment and whole life policies.

post-war period as interest rates have increased. For example, one British actuary at the 1972 international Congress of Actuaries stated[1]:

> Many different bonus systems have evolved to deal equitably with different generations and classes of policies. As yet, however, no British life office has felt it necessary to award a bonus to policy-holders with non-profit contracts taken out many years ago subject to premiums calculated on much lower rates of interest than those subsequently earned. It was the emergence from non-profit business of a similar surplus of embarrassing size in the nineteenth century which caused the birth of the with-profit contract. Now the with-profit policy-holder reaps the whole benefit of these higher interest earnings . . . I consider there is a strong case in equity for the non-profit policy-holder whose policy was issued before about 1950 to receive some of the benefit from this major change, which could not have been foreseen when the contract was effected. At present, he receives a demonstrably poor bargain.

In the United States it seems that as many as 20 per cent of ordinary branch policies lapse in the first two years. Reported lapse rates in the United Kingdom are not so high. Patrick and Scobbie (1969) estimated the rates of lapses in the United Kingdom (from 1965 data supplied by five companies) to be 6 per cent in the first year, 23 per cent in the first five years and 33 per cent in the first ten years. Policies with small premiums tend to have high lapse

[1] *19th Congress of Actuaries*, Vol. I, p. 393.

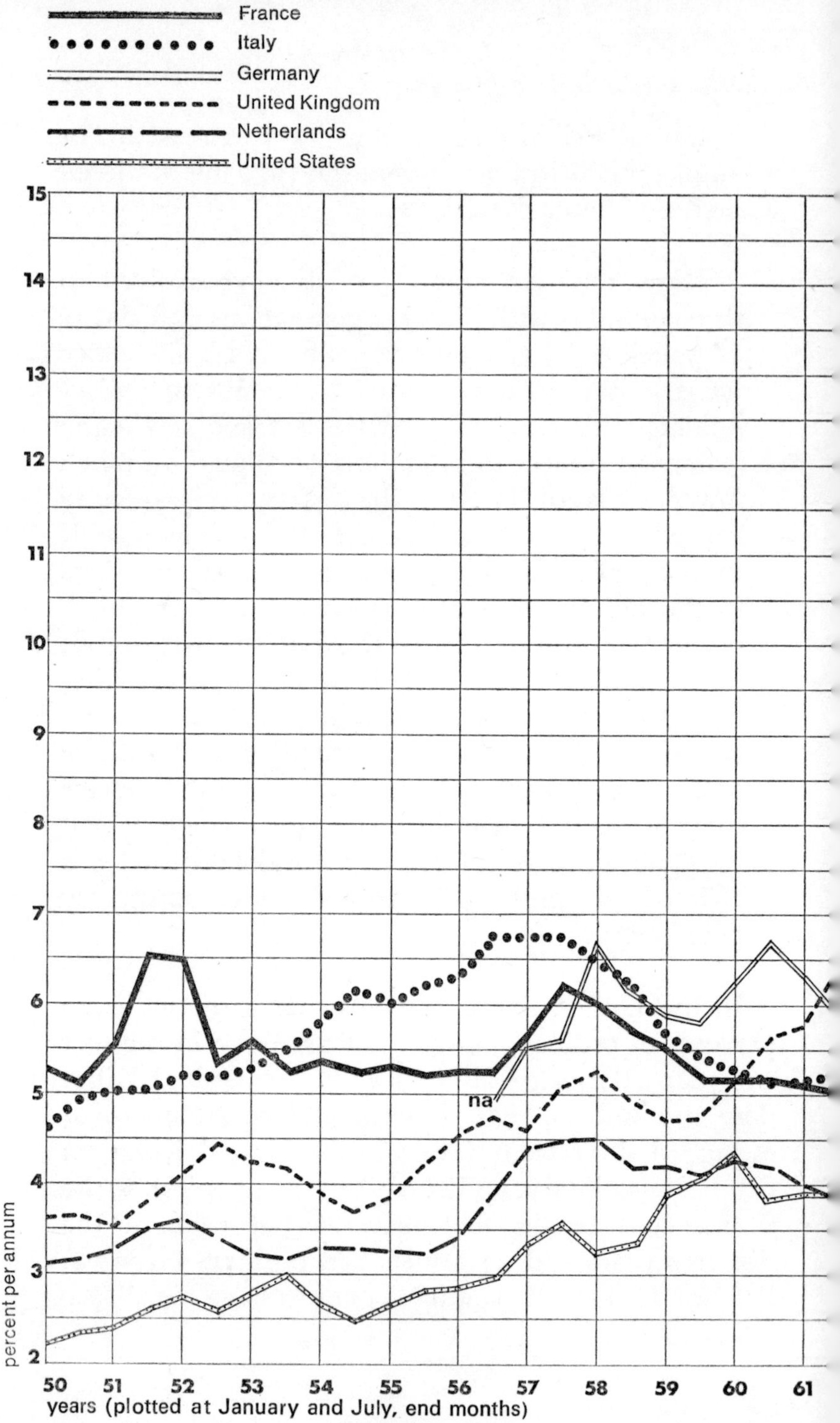
France
Italy
Germany
United Kingdom
Netherlands
United States
15
14
13
12
11
10
9
8
7
6
5
4
3
2
percent per annum
na
50
51
52
53
54
55
56
57
58
59
60
61
years (plotted at January and July, end months)

DIAGRAM 10

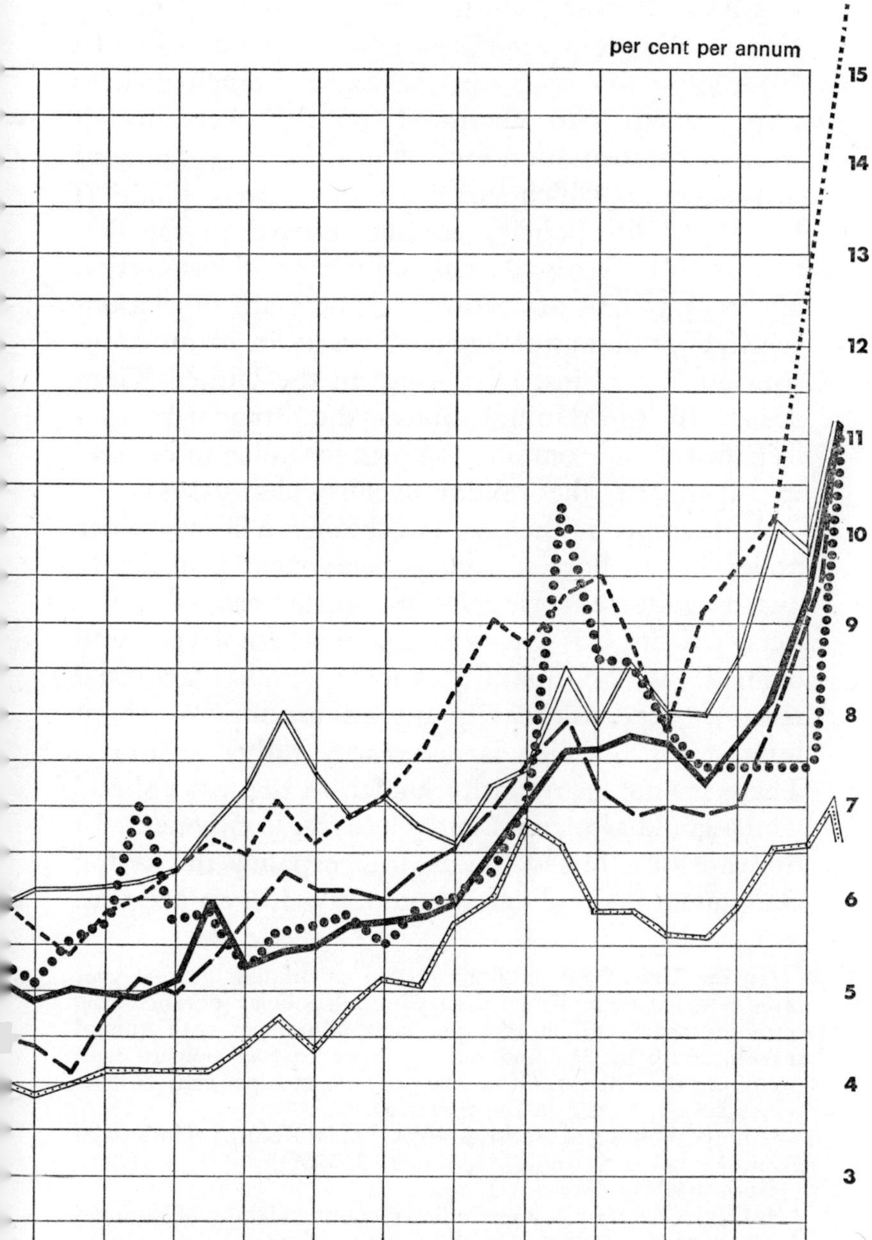

THE YIELD FROM LONG-TERM GOVERNMENT BONDS IN SIX COUNTRIES: 1950–74

rates,[1] and most industrial branch policies in the United Kingdom appear not to reach maturity. In 1972, 3579 thousand new industrial branch policies were issued, 618 thousand policies were forfeit without compensation and there were 2143 thousand surrenders for which surrender values were paid.[2] If traditional life policies are surrendered in the first two or three years at most only a small proportion of the premiums are returned. There are regulations specifying minimum surrender values in many countries and for industrial policies in the United Kingdom.[3] In the United States the Standard Non-forfeiture Law[4] contains complex formulae to be used in calculating the minimum surrender values.

As described in the previous chapter, a life assurance policy has to have a savings component in order to guard against adverse selection. In the case of traditional policies this saving component is not very well defined, as the quantity known as the 'actuarial reserve' depends heavily on an assumption about interest rates, which is necessarily rather arbitrary. There is another quantity known as the 'asset share' which could also represent the saving component. In the case of a linked life assurance policy the saving component is simply an amount saved in an account,

[1]In the United States, Buck (1960) calculated the first year lapse rates for a sample of ordinary branch policies (not including term insurance) to be 16·1 per cent of policies with annual premiums up to $50 and only 3·1 per cent of policies with premiums over $1000. Of all the policies, 11·4 per cent of male policy-holders lapsed in the first year.

[2]Annual Abstract of Statistics, 1974, Table: Returns of industrial assurance taken up and discontinued, HMSO.

[3]Industrial Assurance Act, 1923.

[4]Effective from 1948, it embodied recommendations of National Association of Insurance Commissioners (1941).

and this can be a bank account, the units of a unit trust or simply a collection of securities chosen by the policy-holder. On surrendering the policy, the policy-holder receives this saving component, less, on occasion, a surrender charge to guard against adverse selection which, together with the charge for the insurance component of the policy, should be predetermined. This type of policy overcomes the difficulties of surrender values and bonuses inherent in traditional policies, from which follows the general principle of allowing life insurance to be attached to saving schemes based on different kinds of means of saving. In the United Kingdom there are linked life assurance policies with the savings component in building society accounts, unit trusts or internal insurance funds. However, in the United States it is not possible to sell linked life assurance policies. There, most proposed 'variable life insurance' policies do not have a savings component which is both clearly defined and visible to policy-holders and, therefore, have no advantages for policy-holders compared to linked life assurance policies, that is, designs of policy which are like saving schemes with an attached insurance component.

It may be asked why the United States do not adopt the linked life policies of the English design which are much less complex than the variable life insurance policies. Part of the answer to this question relates to the regulatory controls on life insurance business. In developing new products life insurance companies naturally seek to include those products under those regulations which will provide them with competitive advantages compared to other saving media. However, if the new products closely resemble the saving schemes of other financial institutions, then it is clearly more difficult for special regulations to apply which do not also apply to other saving media. This is a reason for the development of the designs of variable life insurance policy, which may be introduced in the near future, in the United States. Life insurance companies are supervised by the state insurance departments whereas mutual funds are supervised by the Securities and Exchange Commission, and the funds supporting variable life insurance will be included under their jurisdiction. However, a large part of the rules applicable to mutual funds will not apply, particularly rules concerning the maximum commission payments to brokers.[1] The control of life insurance companies in the United Kingdom is much more informal than in the United States, where there are detailed regulations governing every aspect of the business (although they vary between states), such as permitted investments, the valuation of investments, the size of surpluses, the distribution of surpluses, the size of commissions, the size of surrender and paid-up values and the provision of loans to policy-holders including the rate of interest paid. This makes the introduction of new designs in the United States a prolonged process. It

[1]The expense charges of mutual funds are not fully prescribed like those of unit trusts in the UK. However, the National Association of Securities Dealers has submitted a formal proposal that the maximum 'sales load' should be fixed under the Investment Company Act at from 6·25 to 8·5 per cent of the offer price. Section 27 of this act (amended 1970) contains rules on front end loading of sales charges for contractual saving plans. Up to 50 per cent of the sales load can be deducted from the first year's payments, but there is a forty-five-day refund period in case the saver has second thoughts and an eighteen-month period in which, if a refund is requested, the sales load over 15 per cent must be returned.

also means that designs of variable life insurance policy in the United States tend to have complex features to be compatible with the regulations for traditional policies.

A reason for the low surrender values of most life assurance policies in the first years is the heavy initial expenses due to the payment of commissions to brokers.[1] A recent government report in the United Kingdom on linked life assurance contains the following passage on the 'front end loading' of expenses charges:[2]

> The particular point of front end loading was raised in evidence. In many schemes the life company deducts a higher proportion of the annual premiums in the early years of a policy than in the later years. For example the percentages deducted might be 60 per cent of the premium in the first year, 25 per cent in the second year, and 10 per cent in subsequent years. In this way life companies are provided with funds to meet the substantial immediate costs which they incur in selling and issuing the policy.
>
> It was represented to us that this system should be, if not prohibited, at least severely restricted since it considerably reduces the rate of growth of the policy-holder's investment during the early years of the policy, and on the grounds that the availability of funds to meet expenses in the early years of a policy may tempt life companies to be

[1]The standard initial commission in the UK is 2 per cent of the sum assured and in the USA it is 55 per cent of the first year's premium with about a further 25 per cent in the next two years' premium (depending on the type of policy).

[2]*Scott Report* (1973), p. 47.

insufficiently strict in controlling these expenses. We are unable to accept this suggestion.

This question of front end loading of expenses occurs with contractual saving schemes in general. In the United Kingdom life assurance policies are at a competitive advantage compared to saving schemes based on unit trust shares, because of their ability to provide substantial first year commissions through the front end loading of expenses. This would no longer be the case if, as suggested, qualifying life assurance policies no longer have to contain an insurance component. The problems associated with the regulation of expenses charges for a saving scheme are greatly increased by the existence of an insurance component, and it is recommended, therefore, that saving schemes or saving media should not have to contain an insurance component in order to qualify for tax concessions, or otherwise to come under special regulations. Single premium linked life assurance policies in the United Kingdom, such as property bonds, have to contain an insurance component in order to qualify as life assurance policies, but there is no specified minimum to this component. It is generally minimal (see 2 in Table V), and it is suggested that this requirement be retracted.

CHAPTER 4

Neutrality of Tax Regulations between Life Assurance and Savings Schemes

Tax concessions for life assurance premiums go back many years. In fact when income tax was introduced into the United Kingdom under Prime Minister Pitt in 1799, life insurance premiums were made fully deductible from income before tax. At this date the business consisted mostly of term insurance with whole life policies developing in the early nineteenth century, followed by endowment policies in the late nineteenth century. Thus since very early days there has been a shift towards a greater volume of business for life assurance policies with a larger savings component, this development having been promoted by the tax concessions given to premium payments. In the United States, where life assurance premiums are not deductible from income before tax, whole life policies are much more popular than endowment policies, whereas in the United Kingdom, where substantial concessions are provided for the premiums of qualifying policies, the contrary is true.

Life assurance premiums are deductible from income before tax in many European countries,[1]

[1]Usually up to a certain limit defined as particular per annum amounts of money per family or per taxpayer, e.g. in 1973, in Sweden SK250 is deductible for a single person and SK500

although in Sweden and Finland only nominal amounts are deductible. In Norway and Germany contributions to certain kinds of saving scheme are added to the life assurance premium and the resulting amount deductible from income before tax up to a certain limit. In Norway the deductible amount[1] includes 'tax free bank saving', for regular contributions over ten years, which is reduced to four years if the saving is used for house purchase or improvement, whereas in Germany there are a number of 'special contributions', including life assurance premiums and contributions to schemes for saving towards house purchase, which are deductible from income before tax.[2] In the Netherlands premiums of life policies are not deductible from income before tax.[3]

A problem arising in the development of linked life assurance policies is whether the premiums of these policies should benefit from the same tax concessions as those of conventional policies. In Germany the tax deductibility of life assurance premiums has not

---

for a couple; in Finland Mk90 is deductible for each member of the family; in Belgium certain percentages of income are deductible up to a maximum deduction of FB45 000; in France F1000 is deductible for a single person, F2000 for a couple and plus amounts for each child and half the remainder up to F5000. In Italy premiums can be deducted without limit.

[1]Kr1400 for a single person and Kr2400 for a couple. In Denmark Kr3000 is deductible, this includes special 'children saving' for parents and grandparents saving for their children.

[2]*Sonderausgaben* which include sickness insurance, accident insurance and employee contributions to state social security. These payments tend to absorb a substantial proportion of the maximum amount deductible before tax so that taxpayers may pay considerably more special contributions than the maximum deductible which varies according to marital status and number of children and is DM4200 for a single taxpayer in 1975.

[3]Unless there is an annuity option.

been extended to linked life assurance policies, Linked life polices run over an initial six-year period but can be renewed before the end of this period without evidence of insurability. However, this six-year period is too short to allow the premiums to be eligible as tax deductible special contributions under the existing regulations for qualifying contributions. A contributor to the 1972 International Congress of Actuaries described the reason for the adoption of the six-year contract period as follows:[1]

> The adoption of six years for the length of the contracts has up till now avoided attempts by policy-holders to have the premiums of linked life assurance policies recognised as special contributions and has also avoided an attempt by investment companies to obtain the same concession for their saving schemes. It seems, almost, that the whole system of special contributions for life assurance has come into doubt.

The linked or variable life insurance policies which have been developed in France are of the second type of design discussed in chapter 3, in that they resemble more closely traditional policies than saving schemes with an attached insurance component.[2]

These designs have been developed partly in order to avoid an attempt by investment companies to

[1] *19th International Congress of Actuaries* (1972), Vol. I, p. 493.

[2] Pottier (1971) contains an interesting discussion of the comparative merits of variable life insurance policies and saving schemes. He states (p. 52): 'variable life insurance policies are too often unjustly accused of being saving schemes without any investment income.' There is only a small amount of business for linked or variable life insurance policies in France and Germany compared to the large amount in the UK.

obtain the same tax deductibility of contributions for their saving schemes (with or without a term insurance attachment) as is permitted for the premiums of qualifying life assurance policies.[1] This is the same reason for the lack of tax deductibility of the premiums of linked life policies in Germany mentioned in the above quotation.

The development of linked or variable life assurance has therefore presented problems for the supervisory authorities in different countries, resulting from the differences in the tax treatment of life assurance policies and saving schemes based on unit trusts or open-ended investment funds. Various different solutions have been attempted, one of which is not to extend particular tax concessions provided for traditional policies to linked life policies. Thus in Germany the tax deductibility of life assurance premiums has not been extended to linked life policies. Another solution is to design the linked policies so that they more closely resemble traditional policies than saving schemes with an attached insurance component, a method that appears to have been followed in France and in the development of variable life assurance in the United States. A third solution, which is followed for qualifying life policies in the United Kingdom, is to permit linked life policies to be like saving schemes and to extend the same tax concessions to them but to specify that they must contain a defined minimum insurance component.

However, none of these three solutions is entirely satisfactory. The first solution produces a lack of tax

[1]There is, however, a tax on premiums of 4·8 per cent and certain special saving schemes carry government subsidies not provided to life assurance.

neutrality between traditional and linked life assurance policies; the second has the disadvantage for savers because it promotes designs of variable life policies which do not have a clearly visible saving component and method of calculating surrender values, compared with designs which are like saving schemes with an attached insurance component; the third has the disadvantage that it obliges savers to have life insurance attached to their saving, even if they do not need it, in order to qualify for tax concessions. Another disadvantage of the attachment of life insurance to a savings medium is that it complicates the question of expense charges.

These problems arise because of lack of neutrality between the regulations for life assurance policies and those for saving schemes, especially with respect to taxation. If certain saving schemes were to have the same tax treatment as traditional life assurance policies, and at the same time formed the basis of linked life assurance policies then these problems would be largely overcome. The saving schemes would have to satisfy the following criteria:

1. Contributions to the scheme are included with life assurance premiums in the calculation of income tax liability.
2. The tax treatment of the scheme is as near as possible to that for traditional life assurance policies, for example, with respect to the proceeds in the event of death.
3. Deductions from the contributions to the scheme or the accumulated saving can be made in order to purchase life insurance cover and to provide a commission to the broker, so that the scheme

can be the basis of a linked life assurance policy.

4. The insurance component that may be attached to the scheme in this way is not subject to a maximum or a minimum relative to the saving component.
5. The saving scheme is provided by the widest possible variety of financial institutions.

It was proposed in chapter 2 that qualifying policies in the United Kingdom should not have to contain a minimum insurance component (defined below) in order to receive the tax concession for premium payments. If this minimum rule were retracted there would be saving schemes satisfying completely criteria 4 and, because of the variety of linked life assurance policies in the United Kingdom, criteria 5 would also be largely satisfied.

In the United States 'package' schemes known as 'buy term and invest the difference' exist, but the term insurance policy has to be legally separate from the savings contract. Thus the beginnings of linked life assurance policies exist but development is held up by regulations. Criteria 3 does not apply properly to the saving contract, the term insurance policy itself containing a saving component. This design, therefore is contrary to the principle of a linked life assurance policy where small contributions pay for the insurance cover in small periods of time. Mutual funds sometimes provide life insurance cover for contractual savers under a group credit scheme where the 'credit' is deemed to be the future contributions, so limiting the extent of the insurance coverage, which is contrary to criteria 4.

In the previous chapter it was claimed that from

the point of view of the endowment or whole life policy-holder, there are certain advantages in linked life assurance policies which provide life insurance cover attached to savings accumulating in an account. From this follows the general principle of attaching life insurance savings of different kinds, so that should someone have a preference for a particular savings scheme, this could form the basis of a policy. The savings schemes should, in principle, include savings which are simply a collection of securities chosen by the saver, but held by a financial institution to ensure that regulations are complied with. It is of interest to note that the German *Spar-Prämiengesetz*[1] expressly includes saving of this kind as eligible for a subsidy. Another particular example of a savings scheme to which the attachment of life insurance can be considered is the variable deferred annuity.

The provision of a tax concession for contributions to a saving scheme implies that the saver should not be able to withdraw his saving immediately while retaining the concession otherwise its value as a saving incentive is lost. Three kinds of restriction used to prevent immediate withdrawals are:

1. The compulsory notice period: the saver has to give notice of a withdrawal some period of time beforehand.
2. The compulsory saving period for each contribution: each particular contribution has to be

[1]Provides a bonus of from DM120 to DM480 per annum (depending on marital status and number of children) for savings in the banking institutions or unit trusts. Single contributions have to be saved for six years and regular contractual saving has to last for seven years. Similar bonuses are provided under the *Wohnungsbau-Prämiengesetz* and the *Vermögensbildunsgesetz*.

saved for the same period of time until it can be withdrawn.

3. The contractual obligation to save: regular equal contributions have to be made for a period of time after which all savings can be withdrawn.

The first two kinds of restrictions may be called single premium restrictions as they apply to each contribution independently of the other contributions. The third restriction may be called a level premium restriction. Withdrawals earlier than the time period specified may be absolutely forbidden or discouraged by being subjected to tax or a specially high rate of tax or by the subtraction of a tax concession supplied previously.

In the United Kingdom tax concessions are weighted towards the level premium life assurance policy as opposed to the single premium policy, since only level premium policies qualify for the 17·5 per cent tax allowance for premiums. Qualifying endowment policies must conform to the following criteria:[1]

1. The full term of such policies must be at least ten years.
2. Premiums must be payable annually or more frequently for at least 10 years or until earlier death.
3. The total number of premiums payable during any period of twelve months must not be more than twice the number which would be payable in any other twelve-month period.
4. The total number of premiums payable in any

[1]This summary of legislation introduced in the 1968 Finance Act is taken from Harris (1970).

twelve-month period must not exceed one-eighth of the total number of premiums payable over the whole duration of the policy.

5. The sum which is guaranteed to be payable on death, whenever that occurs, must be at least 75 per cent of the amount of the total premiums which would have been paid at maturity of the policy.[1]
6. The annual premium payments must not exceed 7 per cent of the sum assured.[2]

The sum assured for many qualifying linked life policies is 180 times the monthly premium payment which, it can be seen, is the minimum required.

This tax distinction between single and level premium policies appears to be unique to the United Kingdom. Level premium policies have the disadvantages associated with the front end loading of charges while single premium policies permit a natural flexibility of contributions. There seems to be no logical reason why a major tax concession should be given for contractual saving as opposed to saving in single contributions. It has already been suggested that certain saving schemes should be provided with the same tax concessions as qualifying life assurance policies. One possibility is that single premium policies and saving schemes be included as well as level premium policies and saving schemes, with a

[1]The 1974 Finance Bill specifies a reduction of this 75 per cent, by 2 per cent for each year for which the age of the policy-holder exceeds 55 at the commencement of the policy.

[2]This rule is designed for whole life and term policies. It is retracted in the 1974 Finance Bill and replaced by a 75 per cent rule. Specifically, the sum assured for qualifying whole life policies must be at least 75 per cent of the total premiums which would be payable if death occurred at age 75.

compulsory saving period of, say, five years for the single premium policies and saving schemes and seven years for the level premium policies and savings schemes.

Money can be withdrawn from many saving schemes without loss of concessions in special circumstances. For example, in France the same list of special circumstances applies to certain government subsidised saving schemes: the 1965 long-term contractual saving schemes, the 1967 participation and company saving schemes. These special circumstances are marriage, dismissal or redundancy, retirement, invalidity or death of the saver or his spouse. Similar rules apply under the German *Sparprämiengesetz*. Another special circumstance in some schemes is that of house purchase, which has already been encountered in the Norwegian 'tax free bank saving'.

The reduction of the rate of return provided by a saving scheme in the event of the death of the saver may be called a 'negative insurance' effect. Such an effect often occurs, for example, with deferred annuities in the United Kingdom when the contributions are often returned without interest or with only a low rate of interest in the event of the death of the policy-holder. It also occurs under the Save As You Earn scheme[1] in the United Kingdom whereby the rate of return is reduced from about 7·2 to 4·5 per cent in the event of death in the first five years. Thus, in this scheme, death is not a 'special circumstance' in the sense used above, since withdrawal of saving in the

[1]Introduced in 1969. This is for regular saving over a five year period with the Department of National Savings, the trustee savings banks and building societies. By the end of 1972 there were just over one million contracts and a total accumulated capital of £199 million.

event of death results in a lowering of the rate of return.

So far in this chapter only tax concessions for life assurance premiums have been discussed. The topic of the taxation of life insurance companies in general is too broad to discuss but nevertheless some remarks should be made. The taxation of open-ended funds is commonly based on the 'flow through' or 'fiscal transparency' principle,[1] that is, the income from the investments of the fund flows straight through to the unit holders and the fund pays no tax itself or is 'transparent' for tax purposes. However, the same principle clearly cannot be applied to the taxation of insurance funds. The income from the investments of an insurance fund has to be able to 'roll-up' to meet claims as they fall due. Therefore the income from the investments of life insurance companies is permitted to roll-up without having to be distributed to policy-holders until policies terminate. There may, however, be rules regarding the distribution of surpluses. The roll-up of investment income is of greater benefit to higher rate income tax payers than to those paying a lower rate and, for this reason, the proceeds of life policies (less premium payments) are sometimes subject to income tax according to an 'income averaging' or 'top slicing' formula.[2]

[1]The application of this principle implies regulations to ensure the distribution of investment income, that is its inclusion with personal income for tax purposes. Unit trusts in the United Kingdom cannot retain more than 15 per cent of their investment income (ICTA 1970, S. 359 [e]). Mutual funds in the United States have to distribute 90 per cent of their net investment income. Different rules apply for capital gains.

[2]These formulae, defining the tax on the proceeds in terms of the policy-holders rate of income tax, tend to be rather complex. Such a formula applies to the cashing-in of life policies and deferred annuities in the USA, and to the proceeds of endowment policies except death benefits. It also applies to receipts from

The subject of taxation of life insurance companies has a different appearance according to whether the richer or not so rich policy-holders are being considered. The more prosperous policy-holders are naturally concerned about reducing their tax liability, sometimes giving rise to highly anomalous situations. For example, at one time one-policy life insurance companies existed in the United States. Some Texan oil-well owners transferred the ownership of their wells to life insurance companies of which they were the sole policy-holders. This was probably done to take advantage of the comparatively low rates of tax paid by life insurance companies in the United States on the income from their insurance funds.[1] An anomaly which has arisen in recent years in the United Kingdom is the provision of loans to policy-holders at a zero rate of interest as an alternative to cashing-in a policy so as to aviod 'top slicing', However this practice is not common and is curtailed by the 1974 Finance Bill.

Single premium policies in the United Kingdom are associated with richer policy-holders. In so far as level premium policies are more important for poorer policy-holders they suffer more from low surrender and paid-up values. The figures on page 74 indicate that most industrial policies do not reach maturity, and policies for smaller amounts have higher lapse rates. The proposed extension of the tax concession given for the premiums of qualifying policies to include single premium policies would encourage more people

---

non-qualifying policies in the UK and to the early cashing-in of qualifying policies.

[1]The 'policy-holders' share of the investment income is exempt from tax.

to buy single premium policies. The large amount of money lost by policy-holders due to early surrenders of level premium policies should make the reduction of this loss a political objective overriding the possible political objections to the extension of a tax concession to single premium policies, because they are bought more frequently by the more prosperous.

CHAPTER 5

Equity between the Generations

In the United Kingdom the uniform reversionary bonus system is used by practically all life insurance companies, which means that bonuses are paid in the form of a fixed percentage addition to the sums assured. If the investment performance of the life fund improves then it may be thought that older policy-holders should benefit more from this improvement than younger ones, since they have made a larger contribution to the capital of the fund. However, the size of the bonuses under the uniform reversionary bonus system does not take the duration of policies into account. For this reason, in the United Kingdom in the 1950s, a problem of equity arose as many companies had received substantial gains from rising share prices and dividend payments, leading to the payment of terminal bonuses on a regular basis. In 1959 the President of the Institute of Actuaries, Mr F. M. Redington, advocated the further use of terminal bonuses as follows:[1]

> Current surplus was considerably improved by the actual increase in the equity dividends which had been received in recent years, and by no

[1] *Journal of the Institute of Actuaries* (1960), Vol. 86, p. 24.

> argument could he convince himself that the increase in income could be properly distributed in the form of a uniform bonus. It clearly belonged more to the older policy-holders. Certainly it did not belong to the new policy-holders and still less did it belong to those who would become policy-holders in the future and who would be the main recipients of the benefit if the traditional methods were followed. . . .
>
> He therefore found within himself a number of arguments for special consideration for the older policy-holders whose collective claim in the name of justice was not easy to resist. The claim was made not only in the name of justice, however, but also in the name of mercy, because behind all the factors there lay inflation.

Virtually all companies in the United Kingdom now pay terminal bonuses, which demonstrates how problems of equity between generations of policy-holders can lead to the modification of an existing bonus system. Actually no bonus system is free from such problems because bonuses are positive payments or liabilities to future payments arising from investments, the value of which fluctuates. Consider, for example, the very simple bonus system in which bonuses are paid as a uniform percentage addition to the accumulated contributions and past bonuses, which means that contributions simply accumulate in an account with interest, a system often used for deferred annuity policies. Problems of equity often arise even in this simple situation. If the assets are invested at a fixed rate of interest x, then should market rates of interest increase to a new rate y, the insurance company cannot provide the new rate to all its depositors without realising its investments in order to invest them at the new rate. This is not generally possible without incurring a capital loss and the insurance company, therefore, will have difficulty in attracting money into the accounts earning the old rate of interest. Thus there is a conflict between the 'new money' and the 'old money', known as the 'new money–old money effect'. A result of this phenomenon was that complex 'new money' methods of allocating investment earnings were introduced for deposit administration schemes in the United States in the late 1950s and they are now in general use. The new money is provided with the rate of interest currently received on new investments less charges and tax. Part of the old money is credited with the same rate of interest, generally according to an assumed 'roll over' period which reflects the time it takes to realise old investments and reinvest them at the higher interest rates. The new money–old money effect disappears if x is variable and the use of variable rates of interest for loans has become more common over the years. Building societies in the United Kingdom provide mortgages at variable rates of interest and life insurance companies have expanded their use of variable rates of interest for mortgages.

In order to calculate the size of the premium for a traditional life policy, assumptions have to be made about future interest rates or return from investments, and future mortality and expense costs. The payment of bonuses can be thought of as arising from a conservative estimation of these quantities, and tends to cause the introduction of an extra 'bonus loading' factor into the premium, which is the difference between the size of the premium of a participating policy and the premium of a non-participating policy providing the same initial guaranteed benefits. Under both linked life assurance and variable life insurance policies, the pre-determination of charges implies assumptions about future mortality and expense costs. Excessively conservative charges may be repaid in the form of bonuses, the payment of which is, in fact, a further complication in the New York Life design. In the United States the allocation of bonuses for traditional policies is calculated using the 'contribution plan', and under a 'three factor' contribution plan the total bonus is made up of an 'interest factor', a 'mortality factor' and a 'loading and expense factor', corresponding to the surpluses arising from the respective conservative assumptions about the future. This method does not produce a simple formula for the calculation of the bonus which can be explained to policy-holders; such as a percentage of the sum assured or premium payments.

Life insurance companies have various kinds of 'contingency' or 'surplus' reserves which are declared in their accounts on the balance sheet, in addition to which are 'hidden' reserves which do not appear on the balance sheet but which can be described as surpluses. A large variety of factors influence the size of these surpluses. On the one hand, departing policy-holders like to receive as much of the surplus as possible,[1] but on the other hand substantial surpluses

[1]In the United States there have been court cases resulting from attempts by departing policy-holders to receive an increased share of the surplus. Jackson (1959): 'A large body of cases throughout the years has arisen from attempts to force large dividend payments or to require distribution to a departing policy-holder of his "share" of the surplus' (p. 788).

can be advantageous to policy-holders as they enable companies to invest more heavily in shares and property. In most states in the United States there are regulations, which control the size of surpluses that can be accumulated by life insurance companies by limiting the size of contingency reserves, and which restrict the valuation of assets so as to limit the size of the 'hidden reserves'. These regulations are sometimes severely criticised on the grounds that they have resulted in a lowering of the rate of return provided to policy-holders by inhibiting investment in ordinary shares.[1]

In the United States in the 1950s, employers with deposit administration schemes began to question whether the preservation of money values in accounts was worth the cost of maintaining the surpluses. This led to a variant of deposit administration known as 'immediate participation guarantee', under which the employers' account is credited with its share of investment earnings ('new money' methods are generally used), without the allocations to surpluses required under conventional schemes. The account is adjusted according to the realised capital gains and losses of the assets of the company.

The difference between the market value of the assets and the book value is a hidden 'reserve', which

[1]For example Jones (1962) wrote: 'most life insurance companies are limited by legislative statute in the amount of surplus they can accumulate. During the early 1950s the average ratio of surplus to total assets for the industry was about 7 per cent. Under these circumstances companies could not absorb wide fluctuations in the value of their assets independent of their liabilities without serious threat to their solvency' (p. 132). 'More liberal investment statutes and a more liberal and rational valuation system would contribute to creating an atmosphere in which life insurance companies could take more suitable risks and concentrate more completely upon portfolio yield' (p. 145).

can be quite substantial. For example, in the case of the British Prudential Assurance Company the balance sheet value of the ordinary branch reserves given in the 1971 end-of-year accounts was £1584 million and the market value was stated to be £1983 million. A discussion of valuation procedures is contained in an international study of solvency requirements for life insurance companies by an OECD group of experts, who recommend very cautious procedures. For example for the valuation of property they state the following[1]:

> Recognising that the various national laws and requirements as to the valuation of immovable property in the balance sheets are generally aimed at securing that valuations are made which are distinctly lower than the current market values, the Working Party recommends that member countries continue to ensure that this cautious policy is preserved.

Hidden reserves also appear during the procedure used to calculate the balance sheet value of the liabilities. For each policy in force an actuarial liability known as the 'reserve', is calculated by discounting the value of the future benefits guaranteed for policy-holders, and subtracting the discounted premium payments due under policies less a charge for expenses. In this calculation assumptions have to be made about future mortality experience, charges and investment earnings. The more realistic these assumptions, the more realistic are the resulting liability values. The balance-sheet value of the liabilities is the

[1]OECD (1971), p. 49.

sum of these actuarial liabilities. The valuation rate of interest used in the calculations for discounting future liabilities is generally very conservative, in that it is considerably less than a realistic assessment of future investment earnings (after tax). This means that the balance sheet value of the liabilities is considerably greater than it would be with a more realistic assumption. These valuation rates of interest, which are generally about 3 per cent, are often subject to specified maxima by the government control authorities. For example in Germany (in 1971) the maximum for life assurance business is 3 per cent, and in most states in the United States it is about 3½ per cent, and the British Prudential Assurance Company uses valuation rates of interest of not more than 3 per cent for ordinary domestic life assurance business. The difference between the balance sheet valuation of the liabilities and the value recalculated using a more realistic rate of interest is another hidden reserve. The relative sizes of the various kinds of reserves for a hypothetical life insurance company are illustrated in diagram 11. This company is assumed to use the following formula in the presentation of its accounts: balance sheet value of assets–balance sheet value of liabilities=contingency reserves+surplus distributed to share holders+surplus 'carried forward unallocated'+surplus distributed to policy-holders.

The effect of a change in the valuation rate of interest on the balance sheet value of the liabilities has been calculated for several British companies by Wood, Mackenzie and Co.[1] The results of some of

[1]Wood, Mackenzie and Co., 68–73 Queen Street, Edinburgh, are members of the Scottish stock exchange. They produce reports on a variety of topics for their clients; table VII is from a 1971 study.

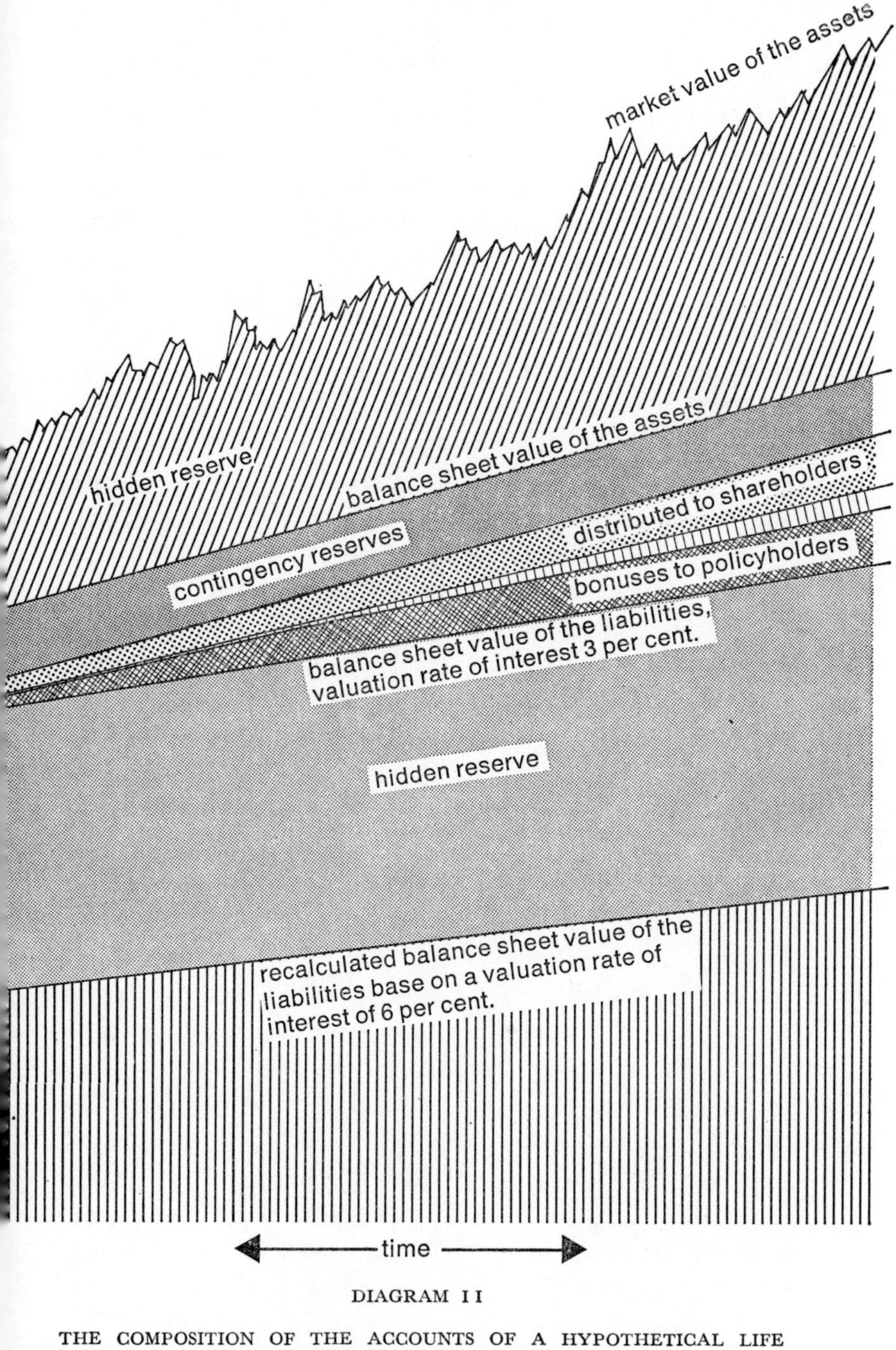

DIAGRAM II

THE COMPOSITION OF THE ACCOUNTS OF A HYPOTHETICAL LIFE INSURANCE COMPANY

their calculations for one particular company are illustrated in table VII. It can be seen that the effect of a change from 3 per cent to $5\frac{1}{2}$ per cent in the valuation rate of interest reduces the balance sheet liabilities for the non-participating whole life policies from £30·6 million to £4·5 million. Using a valuation rate of interest of 6 per cent this probably will become negative which means that there is no future liability resulting from these policies; instead they represent an asset. In other words, if the non-participating policy-holders continue paying their premiums, which are then invested at 6 per cent (after tax), this capital (with at most a very small initial fund) will be more than adequate to pay the claims resulting from these policies as they fall due. The overall rate of return provided for this class of business must therefore be substantially less than 6 per cent.

In table VII the balance sheet value of the liabilities for the participating whole life policies was reduced from plus £161 million to minus £151 million when the valuation rate of interest was changed from $2\frac{3}{4}$ per cent to $5\frac{1}{2}$ per cent. A factor contributing to this very large change is that the company's valuation does not include the bonus loading portion of the future premium payments. Neither of the valuations take the value of future bonus payments into account.

Policies with all bonus systems tend to be sold in anticipation of, or on the understanding that, the present rate of bonus payments will be maintained in the future. In the United Kingdom insurance companies generally make a valuation for their own internal use known as a 'bonus reserve valuation', which is a valuation of the liabilities including anticipated future bonus payments, and using more realistic

TABLE VII

THE EFFECT OF INCREASING THE VALUATION RATE OF INTEREST ON THE BALANCE SHEET VALUE OF THE LIABILITIES

Ordinary branch business		*Company valuation* Valuation rate of interest	Liability from sums assured and declared bonuses only	(*£ million*) Balance sheet liability[1]	*W. M. & Co. valuation* Valuation rate of interest	Liability from sums assured and declared bonuses only	(*£ million*) Balance sheet liability
Non-participating (without profit)	whole life	3%	88·5	30·6	$5\frac{1}{2}$%	50·2	4·5
	endowment		56·9	28·2		40·9	14·8
Participating (with profit)	whole life	$2\frac{3}{4}$%	530·0	161·0	$5\frac{1}{2}$%	247·8	−151·0
	endowment		927·9	478·9		648·2	121·6

[1]Liability from sums assured and declared bonuses—discounted future premium payments less expenses.

valuation rates of interest,[1] Published accounts do not in general make allowance for future bonuses in the balance sheet liabilities.

To summarise the factors which influence the size of the surpluses the supervisory authorities and managers of insurance companies are most concerned to ensure that the surpluses are adequate to maintain solvency, but the preservation of equity between policy-holders, on the other hand, requires that surpluses are controlled and for this reason they are sometimes subject to legal limitations designed to restrict their size. During the late 1950s and 60s British insurance companies started to 'write up' the value of their assets in the balance sheet with the resulting capital gains and increased dividend revenues providing terminal bonuses. The substantial surpluses that have been accumulated by many life insurance companies have put them in a very secure financial position.

Bonuses arise from traditional business where guaranteed benefits are payable. Many linked life assurance and deferred annuity policies provide guaranteed minimum benefits at specified maturity dates so that whatever the performance of the fund to which the policy is linked the maturity benefit provided cannot fall below a certain minimum. For example, a substantial proportion of all linked endowment policies in the United Kingdom provide a guaranteed sum on maturity which is equal to the total premium payments. Guaranteed rates of return of up to about 4 per cent over ten or more years are provided for some linked policies, and are known as

[1]The Equity and Law Life Insurance Company uses this procedure in its published accounts with a valuation rate of interest of 6½ per cent for life assurance business.

'investment guarantees' or 'investment insurance'.

There has been some questioning as to whether particular investment guarantees are in fact meaningful, in the sense that there is a probability that the guarantee will one day have to be exercised,[1] or whether particular insurance companies have adequate reserves to cover the guarantees. Assuming that the guarantee is meaningful then a charge has to be made to pay for it in the form of small deductions from the premium payments or saving contributions. Attempts have been made to quantify this charge from a statistical analysis of past investment performances,[2] but a problem with practical applications of this work is that a small change in the assumptions produces a large change in the results. Supervisory authorities have become concerned as to whether life insurance companies which provide investment guarantees should set up special funds to cover them, and if so, how large these funds should be.[3] Separate

[1]An article on managed bonds in *Planned Savings* on 30 May 1973 stated, 'It would appear that the guarantees with managed bonds are little more than window dressing and should be treated as such'.

[2]Turner (1970) calculates the charge known as the 'risk premium' to be made for guaranteeing the return of contributions for saving schemes with level annual contributions based on a fund of shares. The yearly investment performance of the fund is defined by the probability density function which best fits the yearly return from Standard and Poor's Composite Share Index over the period 1880–1967. Realistic assumptions are made concerning expenses and withdrawals. For a scheme running over twenty years when the long-term rate of return (mean of the distribution) is 8, 10 or 12 per cent, the risk premium is respectively 2·00, 0·70 and 0·25 per cent of annual contributions. For a 10 per cent long-term rate of return and a scheme running over ten, twenty and 30 years the risk premium is 5·30, 0·70, 0·24 per cent of contributions.

[3]Hickman (1970) gives theoretical estimates of the size of the required reserves. The discussion following this paper is of

charges for the guarantee component for linked life policies in the United Kingdom are not made in practice but instead included in the charge for the insurance component. Therefore proposals already made for changes in the regulations so as to make the insurance component optional would tend to reduce the use of investment guarantees.

As discussed in previous chapters, there has been a general trend towards policies which do not provide future guaranteed benefits or provide, at most, a small guarantee element. However the new State Reserve Pension Scheme in the United Kingdom proposed in 1973[1] was based on the uniform reversionary bonus system and problems of equity between generations were anticipated as can be seen from the following paragraph from the 1973 Social Security Bill:[2]

> When declaring a bonus, the Board may, in so far as they think it equitable to do so –
>
> (a) specify for particular categories of pensioners (present or future) a rate of increase greater or less than the uniform rate; and
> (b) deal differently between categories of pensions (either by specifying different increases or by

---

interest. Canadian guidelines are given, 'For equity-linked contracts with a guaranteed maturity value, a risk premium not less than 1 per cent of the gross premium for the contract, shall be allocated to a "security reserve" within a life insurance fund' (p. 227). *See also* Scott Report (1973), p. 27.

[1]This scheme was subsequently retracted when the Labour Government took office. It was planned to invest the reserves of the State Reserve Scheme mainly in shares.

[2]Social Security Bill 1973, Section 76(5).

> excluding a particular category of pensions from increase) by reference to when the contributions or premiums going to the rate of pension were paid.

This is a group deferred annuity system using single premium funding. The guaranteed future pension provided for each contribution is based on an accumulation at 4 per cent, but because of the bonuses, and as contributions do not accumulate in the accounts, members will not know the year-by-year rate of return provided for their money. It would be no more difficult to provide a 4 per cent guaranteed rate of return using a variable deferred annuity system. The pension provided by a variable annuity policy of the designs described in chapter 3 fluctuates. However, it is possible to provide a guarantee for a variable policy so that, for example, the pension will not fall below the initial value. The fluctuations under the first design described in chapter 3 are quite smooth. It is possible to modify designs to provide smoother fluctuations by, for example, using an average of market prices over two or three years. In the author's opinion a variable annuity system is greatly preferable to a bonus system because of the difficulties with the visibility of rates of return and equity between generations which arise with traditional bonus systems.

Conclusions

As life insurance companies in different countries have in the past had, at most, only a small proportion of their assets invested in shares and property, the rate of return provided by life assurance policies has been comparable with that provided by fixed interest investments. The value of such investments was reduced to practically zero in several countries in the inflations associated with two world wars.[1] The investments of life insurance companies are now more diversified, at least in the United Kingdom, and traditional policies may provide a reasonable or good rate of return compared with other savings media, but only in the sense that they are a better investment than shares when the stock market is declining because the return is partly based on fixed interest investments; and better than fixed interest investments when the stock market is rising because the return is partly based on shares. They did not share to any great extent in the sharp rise in share prices during

[1]During the period 1918–23 the currencies of Austria and Germany depreciated to virtually zero and those of Belgium, France and Italy depreciated to between a third and a fourth of their original value against the pound sterling. Over the period 1938–50 the French franc decreased to a fifth of its original value against the pound and the Italian lira to an eighteenth of its original value. The value of the German mark was divided by ten in the 1948 currency reform.

the 1920s and 1950s.[1] There is nothing intrinsic about life assurance policies which gives them an advantage as a means of savings, except their tendency to be given tax advantages.

As a saving medium traditional life assurance policies suffer from inherent disadvantages compared to most other saving media: they cannot be readily sold to other savers;[2] the rate of return provided is difficult to ascertain; the charges are not defined; the cash or surrender value is low in the first years of the policy and the method by which it is calculated is not clear. For these reasons *tax concessions for life assurance policies, compared with other saving media, are not an efficient way of promoting personal saving.*

The relative amounts of different kinds of business of life insurance companies, endowment policies, whole life policies and group life schemes have been

[1]The Economist Intelligence Unit (1970) calculated the aggregate rate of return obtained from some level premium participating endowment policies for the periods 1920–30, 1930–40, 1940–50, 1950–60, 1958–68 to be respectively 4·6, 4·8, 4·1, 5·8, 7·0 per cent. The specimen policies chosen were amongst the better performers (the value of the insurance component was taken into account but not the probability of surrender) so that the latter figure for an average policy would probably be 6·5. For the periods 1950–60, 1958–68 the returns from a share index (that of de Zoete and Bevan (1974)) with regular equal sums invested were respectively 19·2 and 10·5 per cent and the corresponding returns from a unit trust index were 19·8 and 11·6 per cent, and from a redeemable government bond index 3·4 and 5 per cent. Various comparative studies indicate that rates of return from participating policies in the UK have been better than those in other European countries, OECD (1969).

[2]There is a market for traditional policies which have a large sum assured and not very many years to run until termination, the purchase of which is known as an 'assignment'. The insurance company has to be notified. The purchaser of a whole life policy must ensure that he knows when the insured person dies and will probably have to produce a death certificate. This can present considerable difficulties in practice.

described for some countries in this work. We may conclude that the business for endowment policies results chiefly from the desire to take advantage of tax concessions and that *a more efficient way of promoting life insurance cover is by the encouragement of group life schemes* rather than by tax concessions for individual policies. The increase in many countries in the amount of life insurance in force under group life schemes compared to that provided by individual policies therefore represents progress. The provision of life insurance provided on a group basis can be promoted by making compulsory mortgage protection provided by group schemes and death-in-service benefits for occupational pension schemes.

It is not suggested that tax concessions for life assurance policies be necessarily withdrawn but that *the objective should be neutrality between life policies and other means of saving*. This suggestion implies that *if the premiums of life assurance policies are deductible from income before tax then contributions to some saving schemes should be as well.* It also implies that *there should not be regulations specifying the minimum insurance component which life assurance policies must contain.*

In France, Germany, Holland and the United States 'variable life insurance' policies have been developed which do not resemble saving schemes with an attached insurance component as do 'linked life assurance' policies in the United Kingdom. *These variable life insurance policies have no merits for policyholders compared with policies in which premiums accumulate in an account as saving and there are specified charges to pay for the insurance component.*

References

Beard, R. E., Pentikäinen, T. and Pesonen, E., *Risk Theory*, Methuen, London (1969).

Belth, J. M., *The Retail Price Structure in American Life Insurance*, Indiana University (1966).

Belth, J. M., 'The impact of lapse rates on life insurance prices', *Journal of Risk and Insurance* (1968), Vol. XXXV. No. 1, p. 17.

Buck, N. F., 'First year lapse and default rates', *Transactions of the Society of Actuaries* (1960), Vol. 12, p. 258.

De Zoete and Bevan (annual), *Equity and Fixed Interest Investment*, London (1919–74).

Die Deutsche Lebensversicherung (annual), Verband der Lebensversicherungs-Unternehmen, Bonn.

Economist Intelligence Unit, *Returns from Investment* 1919–1968, The Economist, London (1970).

EEC Commission, *The Development of a European Capital Market* (1966), Chairman: Segré, C.

Eurofinance (1971), *The Major Life Insurance Markets of Western Europe*, mimeograph, Eurofinance, Paris (1971).

Fellows, D. E. 'Insured group pension plans and ancillary benefits', *Journal of the Institute of Actuaries* (1972), Vol. 99, Part 1, p. 412.

Ferrari, J. R., 'Investment life insurance versus term insurance and separate investment', *Journal of Risk and Insurance* (1968), Vol. XXXV, No. 2, p. 181.

Fraser, J. C., Miller, W. N. and Sternhill, C. M., 'Analysis of basic actuarial theory for fixed premium variable benefit life insurance', *Transactions of the Society of Actuaries*, 1969 Annual Meeting Number, p. 343.

Greenough, W. C., *A New Approach to Retirement Income* (fourth printing), Teachers Insurance and Annuity Association of America, New York (1964).

Gregg, D. W., *Group Life Insurance*, R. D. Irwin Inc., New York (1962).

Handbook on Pensions and Employee Benefits, Kluwer-Harrap Handbooks in association with the National Association of Pension Funds (1973).

Harris, P. and Hewson, D., *Life Assurance and Tax Planning*, Sweet and Maxwell, London (1970).

Hickman, H. W., 'A reserve basis for guaranteed benefits under variable annuity contracts', *Transactions of the Society of Actuaries* (1970), Vol. 22, p. 191.

Institute of Life Insurance, *Report of the Committee to Study Non-forfeiture Benefits and Related Matters* (1941), Committee of the National Association of Insurance Commissioners, New York.

Institute of Life Insurance, *Report of the Joint Special Committee on Life Insurance Costs* (1970), American Life Convention and Life Insurance Association of America, New York.

Insurance Institute of London, *Life Assurance and Pensions in the European Community*, Report by Advanced Study Group No. 200 (1972), Leader Clark, K.

19th International Congress of Actuaries (1972), *Life and pension insurance with variable sum assured and variable premium*, Vol. 1 of the transactions.

Jackson, R. T., 'Some observations on ordinary dividends', *Transactions of the Society of Actuaries* (1960), Vol. XI, p. 764.

Johnson, G. E., *Variable Annuities*, Reprint Company Inc., Washington, D.C. (1971).

Jones, L. D., *Investment Policies of Life Insurance Companies*, Harvard University (1968).

Leckie, H. S., 'Variable annuities and variable life insurance in the United States of America', *Journal of the Institute of Actuaries* (1972), Vol. 20, Part 2, p. 69.

Life Insurance Fact Book (annual), Institute of Life Insurance, New York.

McGill, D. M., *Fundamentals of Private Pensions*, R. D. Irwin Inc., University of Pennsylvania (1964).

McGill, D. M., *Life Insurance*, R. D. Irwin, Inc. (1967).

OECD, *Capital Markets Study*, Committee for Invisible Transactions, OECD, Paris (1967–8).

OECD, Invisibles Committee, *Study on Life Assurance and Private Contractual Savings*, mimeograph. Paris (1969).

OECD, *Financial Guarantees required from Life Assurance Concerns*, Paris (1971).

Patrick, F. D. and Scobbie, A., 'Some aspects of withdrawals in ordinary life business', *Transactions of the Faculty of Actuaries* (1969), Vol. XXXI, p. 53.

Planned Savings, (monthly), Wootten Publications, London.

Pottier, M., 'Les contrats à capital variable', *Argus*, 8th January 1971, p. 50.

Scott Report, *Linked Life Assurance*, Report of the Committee on Property Bonds and Equity-Linked Life Assurance, HMSO, London (1973).

Securities and Exchange Commission, *Institutional Investor Study Report*, U.S. Government Printing Office, Washington (1971).

Turner, S. H., 'Asset value guarantees and equity-based products', *Transactions of the Society of Actuaries*, 1969 Annual Meeting Number, p. 459.

Wharton School of Finance and Commerce, *Proceedings of the National Conference on Variable Life Insurance*, University of Pennsylvania (1971).

Sources of Data for Diagrams and Tables

DIAGRAMS

1. UK: *Financial Times* industrial ordinary share index, plotted without a change of scale. Other countries: *International Financial Statistics*, January and July figures (end months), USA: Standard and Poor 500 ordinary share index, Italy: 'general' share prices.
2. Internal funds: author's estimate. Other data: *Annual Abstract of Statistics*. Life insurance companies: 'life and annuity funds' of ordinary business plus 'industrial assurance funds'. Trustee savings banks: ordinary and special investment departments.
3. Private sector pensions, state and local authority pensions, insured pension schemes, separate accounts: *Life Insurance Fact Book*. Mutual funds 1952–60: Securities and Exchange Commission (1971). Other data: *Federal Reserve Bulletin.*
4. Open-ended property companies and open-ended investment companies (Kapitalanlagegesellschaften, Aktienfonds): *Monthly Report of the Deutsche Bundesbank* respectively January 1973, March 1963 and Statistisches Beiheft (Reihe) of December 1973. Other data: *Statistiches Jahrbuch für die Bundesrepublik Deutschland;* the Table headed 'Aktiva und Passiva der Kreditinstitute' and 'Bausparkassen, Spareinlagen': GNP is 'Bruttoinlandsprodukt'. Data about pensions has not been included because of the comparative lack of funded pension schemes similar to those in the UK and USA.
5. *Annual Abstract of Statistics*. Insurance companies.: table entitled 'Balance sheets: Assurance companies (life and other) established within Great Britain'.
6. Private pensions funds, state and local authority pension funds: Securities and Exchange Commission (1971), Supple-

mentary Vol 1. Life insurance companies: *Life Insurance Fact Book*.

7. Linked life assurance: Scott Report (1973), p. 82. Other data: *Annual Abstract of Statistics*.
8. *Life Insurance Fact Book*.
9. *Life Insurance Fact Book*.
10. *International Financial Statistics*, January and July figures (end months). Germany: 'mortgage bonds'.

TABLES

I. USA and Canada: *Life Insurance Fact Book*. Other countries: 1972, *Die deutsche Lebensversicherung* (1974); 1950 and 1960, OECD (1969) Part II, table A–4. A few figures are from *Transactions of the International Congress of Actuaries*.

II. *Transactions of the 19th International Congress of Actuaries* (1972), Vol. 2, 'The government control and supervision of the private insurance industry'.

III. USA and Canada: *Life Insurance Fact Book*, USA not including group credit insurance. France and Sweden, 1969: *Die deutsche Lebensversicherung* (1971), p. 54. France 1950 and 1960: Insurance Markets of the World, 1964, Swiss Reinsurance Company, p. 57. Sweden 1950: *Transactions of the 15th International Congress of Actuaries*, 1957, Vol. I, p. 482.

IV. USA and Canada: *Life Insurance Fact Book*. Germany and 1972 data: *Die deutsche Lebensversicherung* (1974), p. 62. 1955 and 1960: OECD (1969) Part 1, Appendix D-19. Some further sources were used and there is some slight incompatibility between sources due to technicalities such as the difference between 'in the United States' and 'in US life insurance companies' (the given data refers to the latter).

V. Column 3: The 'Fair Share Whole Life Plan' of Lloyd's Life Assurance Limited.

VI. Life Assurance (1971), Wood, Mackenzie & Co., 68–73 Queen Street, Edinburgh. Investment research report for private circulation, data used by permission.

Index and Glossary of Terms

The initials UK and USA indicate that a term is used or is applicable in only one of these countries.

Annuity: an income or pension for a specified period of time or the contract for such an income. A deferred annuity. *See:* Deferred annuity, Group deferred annuity, Variable annuity.

Assurance (UK): within the British life insurance industry the term 'life assurance' is used and not 'life insurance', according to the convention that 'assurance' is for a fixed amount whereas the pay out under an 'insurance' policy is variable, depending on the extent of the damage. However, in the UK the term 'life insurance' is common and is used in this book where 'life assurance' is generally used if there is a substantial saving component.

Bonus (UK): (USA equivalent 'dividend'), an addition to the initial guaranteed benefits for a traditional life policy. This may take the form of: an increase to the sum assured; a reduction in premium payments; a cash payment; an accumulation in an account with interest; an increase to the term of the policy (for term insurance); a reduction in the term of the policy (for endowment assurance). The first four are common in the USA and are used in roughly equal proportions. *See*; bonus loading, contribution plan, participating policy, reversionary bonus, terminal bonus.

Bonus loading: an addition to the premiums of participation policies which results in a higher premium than that which would otherwise be required to provide the same initial guaranteed benefits with the same actuarial assumptions, 94

Contribution plan (USA): a method of calculating bonus payments in the United States and used in some other countries such as Canada, Germany, Sweden, 95

Variable life insurance (USA): policies in which the face amount (sum assured) and cash value is directly linked to the performance of an investment fund, 55, 58, 75, 82, 108

Whole life policy: a policy in which a particular sum is paid in the event of death whenever occurring.
compared with endowment policy, 29, 33, 79